CELEBRATION OF S

Kent &

C000218934

Basil Cooper

IAN ALLAN Publishing

Title page:
Rebuilt 'West Country' Pacific No 34026 *Yes Tor* leaves the sidings at Folkestone Junction with a boat train for Victoria.
D.Sellman

Below:
'H' Class 0-4-4T, No 31308, is seen amidst the Kentish hop fields near Goudhurst with the Paddock Wood-Hawkhurst branch train on 13 May 1961.
D. M. C. Hepburne-Scott/Rail Archive Stephenson

Front cover:
A Ramblers' special is seen at Goudhurst on 28 May 1959 hauled by 'D1' class No 31739. *R. C. Riley*

Back cover top:
'Battle of Britain' No 34066 *Spitfire* and 'Q1' No 33027 both wait at Tunbridge Wells West on 22 March 1964.
Hugh Ballantyne

Back cover lower:
'Battle of Britain' No 34078 *222 Squadron* takes the Dover line at Keamsey Loop with an up Margate-Charing Cross service on 23 May 1959. *R. C. Riley*

First published 1994

ISBN 0 7110 2242 9

Published by Ian Allan Publishing
an imprint of Ian Allan Ltd, Terminal House, Station Approach, Shepperton, Surrey TW17 8AS.
Printed by Ian Allan Printing Ltd, Coombelands House, Coombelands Lane, Addlestone, Weybridge, Surrey KT15 1HY.

Contents

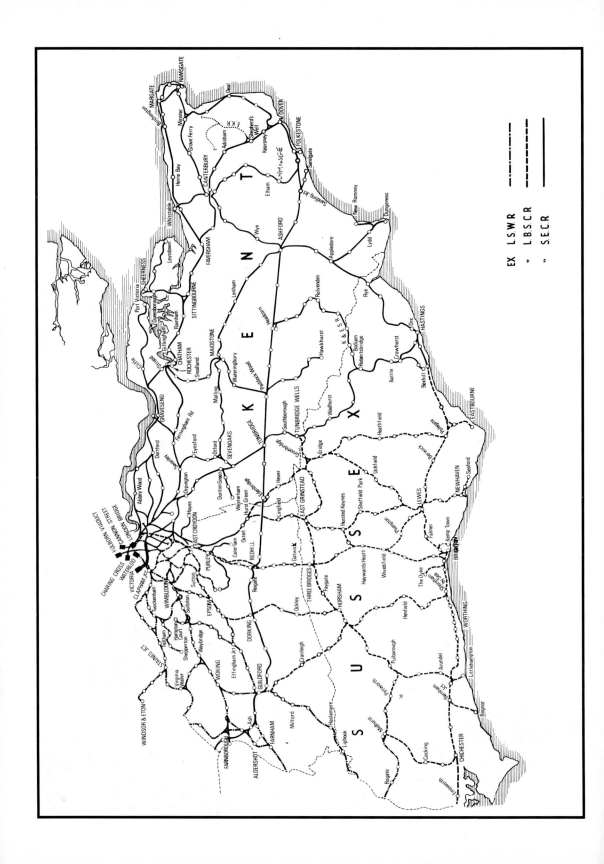

SUSSEX

The Southern Railway's main line electrification turned the London, Brighton & South Coast Railway into a legend overnight. To those who lived north of the Thames the railway was always a curiosity. With virtually no corridor coaches, catering in Pullman Cars, and a partiality for tank engines, the railway hardly conformed with accepted main line standards elsewhere. The 'King Arthurs' after Grouping improved the image a little. Naming had been an LBSC tradition for most of its life and Sir Ontzlake and his knightly colleagues carried it on but struck a new note.

By the time they got down to later members of the class Southern Publicity was beginning to scrape the barrel of the Arthurian legend and sometimes made do with bit players. Sir Ontzlake had a relatively minor role, having been wounded 'through both his thighs with a spear'. On recovering, he assisted Arthur in an abortive attempt to capture the King's enchantress sister, Morgan Le Fay, who had made one of her periodic attempts to kill her royal brother. Predictably she eluded pursuit by turning herself and her retinue into 'a great marble stone'. Arthur and Sir Ontzlake returned home, satisfied that they had witnessed an act of divine retribution. The lady thereupon reconstituted herself and her followers saying 'Sirs, we may now go where we will'.

The names of the Brighton's own locomotives had more mundane associations. Many of them formed a gazetteer of Sussex towns and villages, extending into South Eastern territory in the east of the county.

When the Brighton main line was electrified an enthusiastic shareholder had looked forward to the day when the nation's capital and its premier seaside resort would expand until they met. Happily this did not happen on the Mid-Sussex line which maintained its tranquillity even after electrification as part of the Portsmouth No 2 scheme in 1938. It never achieved the fame of the Brighton line. Its trains disappeared mysteriously from the main line at Streatham and did not reach well-charted territory again until they emerged on the coast line at Ford. I remember returning from a function at Havant with a colleague who lived at Dorking. The rest of our party went back to Waterloo and when I suggested that we wait

Below:
BR Standard 2-6-4T No 80011 shunts its train from the up to the down line at East Grinstead on 15 March 1958.
G. Daniels

for the Victoria train he expressed polite disbelief having evidently thought of his local station only in terms of commuting to London. However, he agreed to the experiment and when in due course an attendant from the buffet car appeared he realised that his home town enjoyed a main line train service.

A steam service continued in the Mid-Sussex area until 1954 and was associated with the early history of the line. A Mid-Sussex Railway Co was authorised in 1857 to build a line from Horsham to Pulborough and Petworth. It was acquired by the LBSC in 1862. At Hardham the line was only a short distance from the coast line at Ford. In 1860 the LBSC was given leave to build a Mid-Sussex Junction line from a junction at Hardham to Ford. It was opened in 1863 and shortened the journey from London to Portsmouth by 10 miles compared with the previous route via Brighton. It may be noted that remains of a Roman posting station on Stane Street were found near the junction. The Romans took their road to Chichester over the Downs at Bignor Hill but the railway followed the easier route down the Arun valley.

In 1859 a Mid-Sussex & Midhurst Junction Co was authorised to build a line from Petworth to Midhurst. When a line from Midhurst to Petersfield was proposed it was at first suggested that it should be built by the LBSC. It was then decided that this might be construed by the London & South Western as an invasion of its territory. In the end the line was built by an independent company under strict instructions that there should be no connection with the LBSC at Midhurst. None the less, a connection with somewhat limited traffic capacity was built later for exchanging wagons and eventually through passenger trains ran between Pulborough and Petersfield, but with long waits at Midhurst. The service continued until the whole line from Hardham Junction to Petersfield was closed in 1954. From 1948 the trains were worked by ex-LSWR 'M7' tanks but the last of Stroudley's 'D1' tanks, No 2552, appeared on the line at intervals until shortly before it was withdrawn in 1950.

The 'D' (later 'D1') tank kept the Stroudley tradition alive among the EMUs in this area of Sussex. It was a versatile 0-4-2T, excellent for suburban and country passenger traffic while being able to take its turn on fast trains and excursions when required, subject to the schedules allowing stops for water. The large-diameter trailing wheels were a distinctive feature being only 1ft less than the 5ft 6in drivers. Later 4ft 6in became the standard for Stroudley's locomotive trailing and tender wheels. A similar general-purpose philosophy guided the choice of EMUs rather than loco-hauled trains when the Brighton main line was electrified. The company Chairman explained that it would enable suburban stock to be brought into use for extra excursion traffic to the coast at weekends.

Travellers on the Brighton main line in the 1950s had a glimpse of steam at Three Bridges when a train for East Grinstead was waiting at a platform on the down side. Bridges were hardly a prominent feature of the landscape but the name of the junction may have come from an ancient document authorising the 'new making of three bridges on ye weyes between ye hamer at Worth and Crawley'. This had been the heart of the Sussex iron industry in the 16th century. The 'hamer at Worth' was probably the Blackwater Green forge in the parish of Worth. Its site has been identified south of Three Bridges station in the angle between the main line and the East Grinstead branch. On the West side of the line, nearer Crawley, the site of the Tilgate furnace is still remembered in the name of Furnace Farm. The bridges were built to ease the way for teams of oxen dragging wagons loaded with iron from the furnace for forging at Worth.

Steam survived on the branch into 1963 when most services were taken over by three-car DEMUs from the Oxted line. In the late 1940s a Marsh tank might be seen but later the line was worked by ex-LSWR 'M7' 0-4-4Ts or ex-SECR Class H tanks of the same wheel arrangement.

Most steam trains from Brighton served the network of lines east of the main line which had been built to establish the LBSC in an area which might be vulnerable to penetration by the South Eastern. Trains to London via the Oxted line travelled from Lewes via Horsted Keynes and East Grinstead (the 'Inner Circle') or branched at Barcombe Mills to take the line via Uckfield and Eridge (the 'Outer Circle'). Some interesting reshuffles of coaches took place at Eridge. A London via Oxted train would detach a portion for Tunbridge Wells which would be taken forward by a train from Eastbourne, while the train from Eastbourne would hand over coaches for the Oxted line.

The 'Inner Circle' was to become famous when BR proposed to close the East Grinstead-Lewes section on 13 June 1955. A rail strike intervened and the last trains ran on 28 May. Research by a local resident, Mrs R. E. M. Bessemer, disclosed that the original Act of the Lewes & East Grinstead Railway required the company to run four trains each way calling at certain stations. The British Transport Commission (forerunner of the British Railways Board) made its own study of the Act and found a loophole in that some stations on the line were not specified as compulsory stopping places. A train service was resumed serving the stations mentioned by name but the trains ran only for a fairly short period in the middle of the day and without reference to convenient connections. This grudging service was kept going for 19 months at the end of which it had been demonstrated to the BTC's satisfaction that the line was hopelessly unremunerative.

In a new move towards closure a three-day public hearing was held at Lewes and the figures produced left the CTCC (the Central Transport Consultative Committee) no alternative but to recommend that the line be closed. The last day of operation was 16 March 1958. At 4.28pm on that day BR standard 2-6-4T No 80154, suitably adorned, left East Grinstead for Lewes with a train strengthened to nine coaches to accommodate a grieving multitude.

The Eastbourne-Eridge line had a long history, entwined with the ambitions of the South Eastern Railway to serve the resort. A branch from the LBSC coast line at Polegate to Hailsham had been opened on 14 May 1849 at the same time as the branch to Eastbourne. In 1873 powers were given to a Tunbridge Wells & Eastbourne company to build a line from Groombridge to Hailsham and in 1876 this undertaking was vested in the LBSCR. Previously the South Eastern had promoted a Bill for a line of its own from Croydon to Eastbourne but this had been dropped in 1864 after an agreement between the Brighton and South Eastern companies on their respective spheres of activity. Construction of the line northward from Hailsham went ahead. It was opened to Heathfield on 5 April 1880 and to Eridge on 1 September of the same year. This was known as the Cuckoo line from the tradition that the first Cuckoo in Sussex was heard each year on the day of Heathfield Fair. The line offered the South Eastern a new approach to Eastbourne. Agreement on the division of London-Eastbourne traffic had been reached between the LBSC and the SER in 1877.

The SER ran a few express trains between London and Eastbourne for about a year but then withdrew them. But through services of a sort lingered on and The Railway Magazine of February 1939 published a photograph of an Eastbourne-Charing Cross train via Tunbridge Wells and Tonbridge at Polegate, headed by an ex-South Eastern Stirling Class F 4-4-0. In postwar years the line carried Tunbridge Wells-Eastbourne trains and a few extras between Hailsham and Eastbourne. Former LBSC classes disappeared from the route in the 1950s and were replaced by Brighton-built Fairburn and BR Standard 2-6-4T. In the end only the Polegate-Hailsham section remained and was served by an Eastbourne-Hailsham steam push-pull which is remembered as slipping unobtrusively in and out of Eastbourne among the EMUs. Hailsham-Polegate closed in the early 1960s.

Shortly after the war the inner and outer circle services still occupied five pages of Bradshaw, the all-lines timetable which could be bought for the equivalent of 12.5p (one's elders spoke of it costing sixpence in their day). Brighton shed provided the engines, usually Maunsell Moguls, Marsh 4-4-2T, or a 'B4X', of which five or six were usually stationed at Brighton at that time. The Brighton 4-4-0s never achieved the fame of the Atlantics. Nominally the 'B4X' was a rebuild of the 'B4' by Lawson Billinton but there was little of the original left. The naming tradition had faded with the arrival of D. E. Marsh but the late A. B. MacLeod recorded two exceptions. When 'B4X' No 52 was completed at Brighton in 1923 it was specially painted and named Sussex at the request of the retiring Locomotive Engineer, Lawson Billinton. This was done in the LBSCR style used for official photographs — matt light grey with black bands and white lining, the lettering also being in white with black shading. There is no record of the locomotive ever having worked a train in this livery, and within a day the lining and lettering were painted over, only the number 52 remaining on a darker grey engine.

The second named 'B4X', No 70, kept its name longer. It was originally Holyrood but in 1907, while still unrebuilt, the name Devonshire was substituted. When MacLeod was Acting Locomotive Foreman at Bognor he noticed that the splashers had been roughly painted grey over the umber livery but the name could still be faintly seen. With a little effort and care the grey paint was removed from the gilt name which was then clearly visible. No 70 was the only 'B4X' to

carry a name while running in traffic. The name remained until the engine came in for a general repair and was repainted in Southern Railway livery.

An interesting 'steam half-hour' could be spent at Lewes station with judicious timing. First the down morning Newhaven boat train emerged from the tunnel and coasted through the sharply curved platform on the 'cut off' line from Keymer Junction which bypassed Brighton for trains to the East Coast line. Steam soared up from the safety valve and there was a haze of smoke from the chimney, soon dispersed as the driver opened the regulator to take his train through Southerham Junction and on to the Newhaven branch.

The level crossing (now gone) at Newhaven Town station was another popular spot to watch the boat train on the last lap of its journey. The Dieppe ferry could be seen towering above its quay lower down the river. At the Harbour station the train would branch on to the short spur leading to the quayside platforms. One had a glimpse of the Atlantic waiting at the shed for its return trip in the evening and of the 'Terrier' (formerly named Fenchurch) which could sometimes be seen trundling over the bridge which carried the road across the upper reach of the harbour.

Fenchurch was bought from the LBSCR in July 1898 for work on the harbour breakwater. It passed into Southern ownership at Grouping. A tram track (grooved) rail was laid on the road bridge crossing the upper reaches of the harbour and Fenchurch used it to reach the harbour branch leading to its working site. Up to World War 2 a man with a red flag walked in front, but in later years, when the weight and volume of road traffic increased, the bridge was closed to vehicles while the train was crossing. Long after the name had been erased, the locomotive was still known to local residents as 'the Fenchurch'. To railwaymen it was 'the tram engine'.

When acquired by BR the engine was numbered 32636. It left its traditional home in 1955 to go to St Leonards for work on the Kent & East Sussex Railway. After a period on the Hayling Island branch No 32636 came to Brighton to share shunting duties, including Newhaven Harbour engine. It was bought by the Bluebell Railway in 1964. Towards the end of steam Maunsell Moguls, and sometimes a 'Schools', shared the boat train workings and the Moguls often headed reliefs following the main train. After the quayside spur was electrified the Southern's Co-Co electric locomotives took over. A relief train would then often be an EMU.

At Lewes, after the boat train had passed, a London via Oxted train soon arrived at the coast line platform, usually with a Maunsell Mogul, to be followed by a Marsh tank bustling importantly though the station although its load was a single van. Inquiry revealed that it was on its way to Glynde to pick up milk tanks for Brighton. I was told by the shed staff at Brighton at this period that ex-South Eastern Wainwright 4-4-0s were frequent visitors on through trains from Tonbridge but none was on hand when I was there.

On one visit to Lewes station I remember seeing the Class J 4-6-2T (formerly named *Abergavenny*) waiting to leave for Tunbridge Wells. A railway picture book in the 1920s illustrated the engine (in ex-works grey livery for some reason) hauling an unidentified train. I have often wondered how many boys grew up under the impression that this was a Great Western engine on that company's North-West route via the Severn Tunnel. But the name had nothing to do with the Welsh station. It honoured a marquess and landowner with connections with the LBSCR Board.

The surviving Atlantics and the Class J tanks were slightly modified by the Southern Railway but their essential character was preserved. The author of the *History of the Southern Railway* published in 1936 (the book was commissioned to celebrate the centenary of the Bodmin & Wadebridge Railway in 1934) was much impressed by these two classes. He described the Atlantic as 'a huge express engine' and the Class J 4-6-2T as 'an enormous tank engine'. He had a superlative in store for the later Class L Baltic tank which struck him as 'colossal'. Under the Southern Railway the 'L' class tanks were later rebuilt as 4-6-0 express engines and went to the Western Section. The 4-6-2Ts were sent to Brighton for scrapping in 1950. Some 40 engines were stationed at Brighton in the late 1940s, a large proportion working on local goods trips and shunting. The number was given off the cuff in the course of an interview. Precise figures for 1949 show a total of 63, still including one Stroudley survivor — a 'D1' tank. Among the engines there were three ex-SECR Class P 0-6-0Ts. These were the origin of intriguing puffs of steam sometimes seen when driving from Brighton to Shoreham.

Beyond the harbour offices the road climbed gently to a bridge. This bridge spanned a single track connecting sidings alongside the coast line on the landward side of the road with Kingston Wharf on the harbour. The 'P' tank moved wagons between the wharf and the sidings but the traffic was small and in 1972 the railway sold the wharf to the Shoreham Port Authority. The line to the wharf was opened in 1870 but was there a link here with an earlier line belonging to the days when the Dieppe packets sailed from Shoreham? A London & Brighton timesheet of 1843 (now in the Bluebell Railway museum) announced that 'the quickest route to Paris is by the railway to Shoreham and thence by packet to Dieppe'. Sailings are listed from 'the railway terminus, Kingston Wharf'. There was a Kingston station on the coast line itself but it was a through station. Perhaps carriages for travellers to the Continent were detached there and sent down to the quayside over an earlier line.

On the coast line west of Brighton motorists waiting at level crossings might be surprised at what turned up instead of the expected EMU. Amid cries of 'Look! A steam train' from the younger generation one of the through trains from Brighton to Bournemouth, Plymouth or Cardiff would sail majestically past. Engines on the Plymouth and Bournemouth services normally worked to and from Salisbury. Normally the Plymouth train had a 'West Country' Pacific but if this was not available Brighton shed might provide a 'Schools', a 'B4X', or a Maunsell Mogul. About 1947 I photographed a 'Schools' leaving Brighton with the Cardiff train, often an 11-coach formation at that time. The Plymouth train was lighter on leaving Brighton but coaches from Portsmouth were added at Fareham. The Bournemouth train was normally a 'Schools' working throughout. A Brighton locomotive allocation list for as late as November 1960 shows three 'West Countries', two 'Battle of Britain' and five 'Schools' at the shed.

At intervals during the day steam was also to be seen on the Horsham branch services. The branch turned inland at Shoreham and made its way via Steyning and Henfield (where a Station Road bears mute witness to the past) to Itchingfield Junction (Christ's Hospital) where it joined the Mid-Sussex line. Old memories go back to Marsh 4-4-2Ts on passenger trains (confirmed by a rather fuzzy photograph taken with a No 2 Brownie camera) but LBSCR survivors in the early postwar years were Billinton Class E4 0-4-2Ts. They were followed up to the closure of the line to passenger services in March 1966 by ex-LMS Ivatt 2-6-2Ts. On some occasions a South Eastern Class H 0-4-4T which had arrived at Brighton on a through train from Tonbridge would fill in time with a Brighton-Horsham working before returning home.

The branch formed a bypass for the London main line south of Three Bridges but it was never electrified and EMUs diverted by engineering works or for other reasons had to travel by the Mid-Sussex line to Littlehampton and reverse. A few London-Brighton steam trains had travelled via Shoreham in the 1930s and one such service was still operating in 1952. It left London Bridge at 5.5am, travelled via Sutton and Dorking, and took 3hr 17min to Brighton with 27 stops en route. There was no corresponding up train and the oddity did not survive. For a short time in the 1960s the 'Regency Belle' charter Pullman train returned to London over the branch in the small hours to avoid weekend engineering works on the main line. Bulleid light Pacifics were the regular power on these occasions but it is doubtful whether the patrons of the service who had enjoyed dinner and dancing at the Royal Albion Hotel, and were now faced with a 'typical English breakfast' at a very untypical hour, were aware of the fact. Except when engineering works made the diversion necessary, the train was formed of a 5BEL set.

Less distinguished locomotives sometimes worked over the line on excursions from the Western Region via Reading which travelled over the Guildford-Horsham branch. They arrived at Christ's Hospital facing in the wrong direction for the junction with the Shoreham branch and usually travelled on to Horsham to reverse, thus passing through Christ's Hospital twice but in opposite directions. Traces used to be visible of a spur off the branch from Guildford which would have formed a triangular junction and avoided this manoeuvre. A Q1 'Austerity' 0-6-0 was seen on one occasion travelling to Horsham at Peasmarsh Junction, near Guildford, with an excursion from Kidderminster.

At one time the branch carried a flourishing freight traffic. All stations except Bramber had yards handling miscellaneous freight and agricultural produce. Industrial traffic came from the Sussex Brickworks at Southwater, which once despatched 40 wagons of bricks a day, and from the cement works at Beeding. After the line had been closed to passenger traffic the 2½ miles from the junction at Shoreham to Beeding were kept open for the cement works. Finally this section was operated as a siding and used for weekly deliveries of gypsum from workings near Battle which travelled via the yards at Norwood Junction and Brighton. The last delivery was received on 21 April 1980.

Much of the shorter-distance freight working on the former LBSC lines was performed by R. J. Billinton's 0-6-2 radial tank engines (radial means that the pivot of the trailing truck was in front of the axle so that the axle moved on the circumference of a circle of which the pivot was the centre). Stroudley had begun the type with the 0-6-2 *West Brighton* which was unfinished at the time of his death and finished by Billinton. In 1863 he brought out the 16 similar engines of Class E3. Although nominally goods engines, their performance on suburban passenger turns led Billinton to introduce Class E4, a modified version built specifically for passenger work. This was a long-lived class still busy in Sussex in the 1960s and working freight as well as the surviving passenger services.

The classic 0-6-0 tender freight locomotive had appeared on the Brighton line in the days of J. C. Craven. Stroudley continued to build the type and R. J. Billinton followed in 1893 with his Class C2. Marsh rebuilt most of the class with a 170lb boiler in place of the original 160lb and a total heating surface increased from 1,211.6sq ft to 1,300sq ft. The rebuilds were classified C2X and they were still a familiar sight on their home ground in BR days. Their appearance had been modified by the fitting of lower cabs and chimneys by the Southern Railway to meet its all-lines loading gauge requirements. When Lawson Billinton succeeded Marsh he fitted some of the class with top-feed apparatus which was enclosed under a second dome. Two domes struck many observers as an oddity and the engines saddled with this excrescence were called 'camels'.

On the London main line, steam continued on inter-Regional services and excursions until dieselisation. The Atlantics shared these duties with 'foreign' classes but in due course gave way to BR Standards. For some time those sufficiently determined in their pursuit of steam could travel behind a steam locomotive on the 3.25am newspaper train from London Bridge to Eastbourne via Brighton. Van trains were another source of steam, worked variously by Billinton Moguls, 'B4X', Marsh tanks or an 'L1' 4-4-0 from the Eastern Section. Brighton shed powered the 6.12pm and 11.28pm van trains to London Bridge, which called at Haywards Heath to pick up vehicles from the East Coast line, and at Three Bridges for those from west of Angmering and the Mid-Sussex line. The 'K' class Moguls, attractively styled with their inclined outside cylinders, have been described as one of the most successful engines the LBSCR ever produced. They were the first Moguls for the LBSCR and the first engines on the line with the Belpaire firebox. Several had Billinton's top-feed apparatus, sometimes under a second dome. Twelve were built and all came into BR ownership.

R. J. Billinton with his 'B4s', Marsh with his Atlantics and six-coupled tank engines and L. B. Billinton with his Moguls and Baltic tanks gave the Brighton line 'important looking' engines, updating its appearance rather as J. G. Robinson had done on the Great Central. There were two classes of Atlantic, 'H1' and 'H2', the latter superheated and with cylinder diameter increased from 18½ or 19in to 21in. A more visible difference was in the line of the platform. In Class H1 it was broken by two small 'humps', one to clear the cylinders and the other at the driving wheels before dipping to the bottom of the firebox casing. In Class H2 the platform rose over the cylinders and continued unbroken until it dropped to below the firebox at the rear of the engine. The only named Atlantic in LBSCR days was 'H1' No 39, *La France*, which gained the distinction in honour of the visit of the French President in 1913. The Southern Railway named both classes after headlands round the coast. Posterity will probably remember best 'H2' No 32424 *Beachy Head* which bowed out with an enthusiasts' special on 13 April 1958.

The longest-lived main line steam service in Sussex was on the South Eastern line from Tunbridge Wells via Robertsbridge and Battle.

At first Hastings was to have been served by the Brighton, Lewes & Hastings Railway, authorised in 1844 and sold to the London & Brighton by the same Act. The line reached St Leonards (West Marina) on 27 January 1846. An extension from Hastings to Ashford

Below:
Ivatt 2-6-2T No 41301 pauses at West Grinstead with the 1.30pm Brighton-Horsham train on 30 April 1964. *J. Scrace*

had also been authorised but the South Eastern had reached Ashford on 1 December 1842 and argued that it could provide a better service from London to Hastings via Ashford than the Brighton line via Lewes. This was agreed and construction from St Leonards to Ashford via Hastings was entrusted to the South Eastern. The line was opened in February 1851 and a service from London to Hastings via Ashford began.

The South Eastern had opened a branch from Tonbridge to Tunbridge Wells on 20 September 1845. There had been pressure for a more direct route from London to Hastings by extending the Tunbridge Wells branch but Parliament had insisted on the Ashford-Hastings line being completed first for strategic reasons, being seen as important for conveying troops across the Romney Marshes in an emergency.

Construction from Tunbridge Wells to Hastings had been authorised in 1845 and the line was completed to Hastings on 1 February 1852. It reached the coast at St Leonards and from there provided access to Hastings for the Brighton company. In a last ditch attempt to delay the opening the Brighton authorities claimed that this stretch of line through the narrow Bo-Peep Tunnel, where single-track working was imposed, was unsafe. They were overruled and later the tunnel was widened. There were still restrictions on some types of rolling stock, however. For many years vans carrying the prohibition were a familiar sight on Southern metals and a constant source of queries in the railway press.

Another tunnel also became well known when its restricted loading gauge stood in the way of meeting the call for heavier and faster trains on the London-Hastings route with more powerful locomotives. This was Mountfield Tunnel, near Battle, which had been lined with only one course of bricks by the contractor. This had to be put right with an extra lining, but it left the tunnel with a smaller cross-section than others on the South Eastern system.

Mountfield Tunnel has linked the Southern's 'Schools' class locomotives indissolubly with the Tunbrige Wells-Hastings line, and in designing them R. E. L. Maunsell had to take account both of its limitations and of the sharp curvature on the route south of Tunbridge Wells. But he was also responding to the brief from management to provide a locomotive of 'Lord Nelson' characteristics but of intermediate power rating and of greater route availability than the 'King Arthur' class.

Two outside cylinders of the size to provide the power required were ruled out by the loading gauge. Maunsell found the answer in cylinder dimensions and valve gear as in the 'Nelsons' but using three cylinders instead of four. The 'Schools' have sometimes been called 'Three-quarter Nelsons'. The baleful influence of Mountfield Tunnel was also seen in the cabsides which tapered towards the top. The boiler was a shortened version of the 'King Arthur' type. A shortened 'Nelson' boiler would have been too heavy and a round-topped firebox was necessary for a good lookout from the cab.

'Schools' dominated the London-Hastings service until the mid-1950s. Their work on the route included some heavy commuter trains, notably the 5.6pm from Cannon Street which, from 1945 until June 1957, was formed of 10 corridor coaches and a Pullman buffet car, giving a tare weight of 358.36 tons. The topography of the route south of Tunbridge Wells ruled out high speed running but there was plenty of hard pulling. The late Cecil J. Allen recorded a run with No 939 *Leatherhead* in the days when the Bexhill branch enjoyed a through service. The train left Hastings with 11 coaches which were taken up the 1 in 100 from West St Leonards after the stop at 36mph. Three coaches from Bexhill were attached at Crowhurst, making the load 344 tons. After restarting from Robertsbridge the engine accelerated to 57mph on 3½ miles of level track and then went up the next seven miles, largely at 1 in 100-132 without speed falling below 39mph. The nominal tractive effort of the 'Schools' at 25,130lb was equal to the 'Arthurs' but the highest of any British 4-4-0.

The DEMUs that were to displace the 'Schools' made some trial runs in January 1957 and began taking over some services in May. With the delivery of buffet car sets the 'Schools' virtually disappeared from the line as from the third week in June 1958. One working lingered on — the 5.45am from London Bridge to Hastings, worked regularly by a 'Schools' until September 1961. The engine returned to Tonbridge via Ashford on stopping trains. Later, 'Schools' alternated with 'N1' Moguls on this service. By the end of 1962 the 'Schools' were gone from the Hastings route. The keenest enthusiast for modern traction could hardly give the DEMUs that replaced them a higher rating than 'dull'.

East of the Brighton Line

The London, Brighton & South Coast Railway sprawled widely over Sussex but 'the Brighton Line' usually meant the main line from Victoria. East of it a web of secondary routes, often built to keep the South Eastern Railway at bay, were still havens of steam in British Railways days. Access from London to this area was from South Croydon over the Oxted line, joint with the South Eastern until LBSC metals were rejoined at Hurst Green Junction or Crowhurst Junction

Above:
'C2X' 0-6-0 No 32440 is at Barcombe with the 12.28pm Saturdays Only football excursion from East Grinstead on 9 April 1955. The train began running on 1 January 1955 for football supporters travelling to matches at Hove. Through tickets were issued from East Grinstead line stations.
A. W. Burges

Below:
With the East Grinstead-Lewes line under threat of closure, 'C2X' 0-6-0 No 32434 with the 3.30pm from Lewes to East Grinstead stands at Sheffield Park on 26 August 1956. A restricted service had been resumed on 7 August.
S. C. Nash

Above:
Class C2x No 32442 heads north near Kingscote with the 9.30am Lewes-East Grinstead service on 14 August 1956 on 14 August 1956. This section of line is currently being rebuilt by the Bluebell Railway as part of its plan to restore services to the line from Horsted Keynes to East Grinstead.
John Head via Brian Stephenson

Below:
Later the same day No 32442 was still running on the Bluebell line. It is seen here nearing the summit of Freshfield bank having just departed from Sheffield Park en route to East Grinstead with the 3.30pm service from Lewes.
John Head via Brian Stephenson

Above right:
No 80011 stands at Sheffield Park with the 12.28pm East Grinstead to Lewes on the last day of operation, 16 March 1958.
J. Scrace

Right:
BR Standard Class 4 2-6-4T No 80065 arrives at Eridge on 9 June 1962 with the 9.10am Tonbridge-Brighton service.
Dennis C. Ovenden

Below:
Ex-LBSCR Atlantic Class H2 No 32426 *St Alban's Head* is pictured at Horsted Keynes on 14 August 1955 with the RCTS's 'Wealden Limited' excursion. Note that this station was served by third-rail electrification over the line towards Ardingly, which can be seen diverging immediately to the left of the signalbox in the distance. Forty years on the Bluebell Railway retains the atmosphere of the steam railway at this station. *D. M. C. Hepburne-Scott/Rail Archive Stephenson*

Left:
Ex-SER Wainwright Class L 4-4-0 No 31778 follows the curve of the Ouse Valley between Barcombe Mills and Lewes with the 3.4pm Tonbridge-Brighton service on 22 August 1956. *F. J. Saunders*

Below:
Class N 2-6-0 No 31868 leaves Eridge for Brighton with the 9.10am from Tonbridge on 6 May 1961. *Dennis C. Ovenden*

GROOMBRIDGE

Above:
The 4.10pm Tonbridge-Eastbourne train arrives at Groombridge on 9 September 1961. No 31876 is a Class N1 2-6-0. *Dennis C. Ovenden*

Left:
C2X No 32447 heads an East Grinstead-Oxted freight at Crowhurst. *A. J. Temple*

Below left:
On 7 March 1960 ex-LBSCR Class K 2-6-0 No 32342, shedded at Brighton (75A), heads towards its home base with the morning pick-up freight from Tunbridge Wells. The train has just departed from Crowborough heading south towards Lewes. *D. M. C. Hepburne-Scott/Rail Archive Stephenson*

17

Above:
Standard 2-6-4T No 80088 leaves Groombridge station with an Oxted line train from Tunbridge Wells on Easter Bank Holiday Monday 1962. *Brian Haresnape*

Left:
The second LBSC 4-6-2T, classified 'J2', differed from *Abergavenny* **in having outside Walschaerts valve gear. It was named** *Bessborough.* **Here it carries its BR number, 32326, and is pictured working the 11.8am Victoria-Tunbridge Wells West train on 2 April 1949.**
Pamlin Prints

Below left:
Fairburn 2-6-4T No 42088 awaits departure from Tunbridge Wells West with the 11.7am to Victoria on 4 September 1958. *A. W. Martin*

Above right:
The 2.55pm Brighton-Tonbridge train headed by BR Standard 2-6-4T No 80150 approaches Groombridge on 9 September 1962. *Dennis C. Ovenden*

Right:
BR Standard 2-6-4T No 80139 brings a Brighton-Tonbridge train into Tunbridge Wells West on 30 July 1960. *G. M. Kichenside*

Above left:
An Oxted-Tunbridge Wells West train leaves Ashurst behind Class H 0-4-4T No 31278. *M. J. Esau*

Below left:
Ivatt Class 2MT No 41326 is seen near Ashurst on 4 May 1963 with a Brighton-Oxted service. *D. M. C. Hepburne-Scott/Rail Archive Stephenson*

Above:
Interchange at Ashurst. Ex-LBSCR 4-6-2T No 32325 arrives with a Lewes portion for Victoria. The 'I3' 4-4-2T on the left has brought in the portion from Tunbridge Wells West. *Cecil J. Allen collection*

Centre right:
Standard 2-6-4T No 80018 leaves Three Bridges with the 4.8pm service to Tunbridge Wells West on 8 April 1964. *J. Scrace*

Below right:
Class L1 4-4-0 No 31784 is photographed hauling a Brighton-Victoria train at Lewes on 10 August 1949. This train was routed over the 'Outer Circle' via Uckfield. *S. C. Nash*

Above:
On 31 August 1949 Bulleid's revolutionary 'Leader' class 0-6-6-0T No 36001 was photographed running through Lewes on a trial run from Brighton to Crowborough. Although work was well advanced on further examples of this remarkable design, No 36001 was the only member of the class to operate. However, in the post-Nationalisation world its life, along with the other members of the class, was destined to be short. *C. C. B. Herbert*

Left:
Standard 2-6-4T No 80034 arrives at Three Bridges with the 4.47pm from Tunbridge Wells West. *J. Scrace*

Below left:
Some found it difficult to take the LBSC seriously as a main line because of its use of small tank engines on main line expresses. Closer acquaintance showed that they were fully up to their work, particularly Marsh's 4-4-2Ts of Class I3. In the early BR years they were still active on secondary routes, but with lighter loads as seen in this picture of 'I3' No 32086. *IAL*

Brighton-Horsham-Guildford

The Southern Railway proposed electrification from Horsham to Brighton in its postwar plans but the work was never carried out. With the branch from Horsham to Guildford it formed a useful cross-country route of more than local interest.

Above:
Class Q1 'Austerity' 0-6-0 No 33025 enters Christ's Hospital on 7 August 1961 with a Reading-Brighton excursion. J. N. Faulkner

Below:
Ivatt Class 2MT 2-6-2T No 41230 leaves Partridge Green with the 4.29pm Brighton-Horsham train shortly before the line was dieselised. G. D. King

Above:
Bramber station on 9 April 1961 with 2-6-2T No 41300 waiting with a Horsham-Brighton train. *S. Creer*

Below:
The 7.40am from Steyning to Brighton leaves Portslade headed by Standard 2-6-4T No 80146. *P. Poulter*

Above:
Billinton 'E4' 0-6-2T No 32512 leads the 3.59pm Brighton-Horsham near Itchingfield Junction on 16 April 1960.
J. Scrace

Below:
Ex-LBSC Class D3 0-4-4T No 32364 at Horsham early in the BR era. The date is 4 October 1949.
IAL

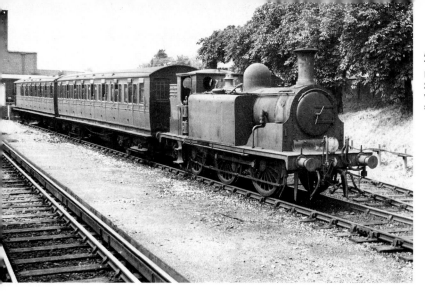

Left:
The last 'D1' 0-4-2T in service, No 2252, is seen at Horsham on 24 June 1950. The locomotive was withdrawn during September the same year. *R. C. Riley*

Left:
The ubiquitous ex-LSWR 'M7' 0-4-4Ts appeared on the Brighton line. No 30050 is near Aldrington on 1 February 1958 with the 1.39pm Horsham-Brighton train.
E. Wilmshurst

Left:
Class M7 No 30053 heads the 9.30am Brighton-Horsham push-pull train between Christ's Hospital and Horsham on 13 June 1969. This locomotive was exported to the United States of America on withdrawal and was later the subject of an appeal to repatriate it. Fully restored in Britain, the locomotive has graced many of the preserved railways in southern England, although nominally based on the Swanage Railway. *J. Scrace*

Right:
Ivatt Class 2MT 2-6-2T No 41287 approaches Christ's Hospital with the 1.34pm Guildford-Horsham service on 24 October 1954.
J. Scrace

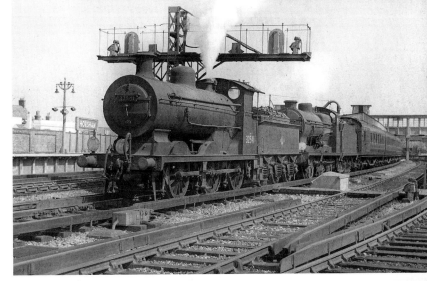

Right:
Class C2X 0-6-0 No 32541 and Class Q 0-6-0 No 30537 are ready to depart from Horsham with the 9.34am ex-Victoria Ramblers' Excursion to Slinfold, Rudgwick and Baynards on the Horsham-Guildford branch on 10 May 1959.
J. Scrace

Below:
Class M7 0-4-4T No 30132 shunts empty stock for the 12.38pm train to Guildford at Horsham on 19 July 1959. *J. Scrace*

Above:
Ivatt 2-6-2T No 41287 approaches Horsham with the 10.34am from Guildford on 7 November 1964. *J. Scrace*

Below:
Ex-LSWR 'M7' class 0-4-4T No 30047 leaves Christ's Hospital with the 11.25am train from Horsham to Brighton on 4 August 1957. *G. Daniels*

Top:
'West Country' Pacific No 34026 *Yes Tor* pauses for water at Horsham with the 11.28am Norbury-Southampton football special on 7 November 1964. The train travelled via Redhill, Horsham and the Mid-Sussex line to Havant. *J. Scrace*

Above:
Another Class M7 0-4-4T, No 30056, pilots 'Q' class 0-6-0 No 30545 leaving Christ's Hospital with a Ramblers' Excursion from Victoria to Slinfold, Baynards and Rudgwick on 4 September 1960. *S. Creer*

Left:
Class Q 0-6-0 No 30546 leaves Horsham with the 9.22am Reading-Brighton excursion on 31 August 1958. *J. Scrace*

Left:
Guildford-Horsham-Brighton provided a tranquil trip by steam through rural England, exemplified in this picture of the midday Horsham-Guildford train shortly after leaving Christ's Hospital hauled by 'M7' No 30050.
Derek Cross

Below:
L. Billinton's Class K 2-6-0s for the LBSCR were primarily freight locomotives but they were a versatile design and did well in other fields. Mogul No 32344 is on a Bank Holiday excursion and is seen leaving Christ's Hospital.
Derek Cross

Selected Shed Allocations

Brighton (75A)
as at 1959

Class M7	30031, 30052, 30053, 30055, 30056, 30190, 30110
'Schools'	30900 *Eton*, 30901 *Winchester*
Class P	31325, 31556
Class L	31776, 31777, 31778
Class K	32338, 32339, 32340, 32341, 32342, 32343
Class C2	32441, 32442, 32449
E4	32468, 32475, 32480, 32484, 32494, 32503, 32504, 32508, 32512, 32515, 32519, 32562, 32577
Class A1X	32635, 32655, 32662, 32670
'West Country'	34008 *Padstow*, 34029 *Bideford*, 34097 *Holsworthy*, 34098 *Templecombe*, 34099 *Lynmouth*
Class 4 (Fairburn)	42066, 42067
Class 4 (BR)	75070
Class 4 (BR)	80013, 80031, 80032, 80033, 80145, 80146, 80147, 80148, 80149, 80150, 80151, 80152, 80153, 80154

Redhill (75B)
as at 1959

Class S15	30835, 30836, 30837
Class N	31817, 31862, 31863, 31864, 31865, 31866, 31867, 31868, 31869
Class C2	32450, 32451
Class 4 (BR)	76053, 76054, 76055, 76056, 76057, 76058, 76059, 76060, 76061, 76062

Horsham (75D)
as at 1959

Class M7	30047, 30048, 30049, 30050, 30051
Class Q	30544, 30545, 30546, 30547
Class E4	32463, 32469, 32470
Class C2	32522, 32526, 32541

Three Bridges (75E)
as at 1959

Class H	31162, 31269, 31530
Class K	32344, 32345, 32346, 32347, 32348, 32350, 32351, 32352, 32353
Class C2	32523, 32527, 32528, 32529, 32532, 32534, 32535, 32536
Class 4 (Fairburn)	42068, 42069, 42070, 42071
Class 4 (BR)	75075
Class 4 (BR)	80010, 80011, 80012

Tunbridge Wells West (75F)
as at 1959

Class H	31278, 31310, 31327, 31329, 31521, 31544, 31554
Class E4	32517, 32581
Class 2 (Ivatt)	41319
Class 4 (Fairburn)	42101, 42102, 42103, 42104, 42105, 42106
Class 4 (BR)	80014, 80015, 80016, 80017, 80018, 80019

Mid-Sussex Line

Although the Mid-Sussex line was electrified in 1938, steam services continued to operate between Horsham, Pulborough and Midhurst.

Inter-Regional trains and excursions brought main-line steam to the Mid-Sussex from time to time.

Above left:
Ex-LBSCR 'D3' 0-6-2T No 2387 waits to leave Midhurst for Horsham in April 1947. *R. A. H. Baxter*

Below left:
A Midhurst-Pulborough train at Midhurst is headed by ex-LSWR 'M7' 0-4-4T No 30110 on 10 April 1951.
G. H. Robin

Above:
'M7' No 30109 calls at Selham with a Pulborough-Midhurst train on 15 June 1954. *J. H. Aston*

Below:
Class U1 2-6-0 No 31894 heads a 10-coach half-day excursion from Princes Risborough to Bognor at Horsham on 28 June 1959. *J. Scrace*

Left:
The 'Midhurst Belle' Railtour, organised jointly by the Locomotive Club of Great Britain and the Railway Correspondence & Travel Society is on the Pulborough-Littlehampton leg of its journey on 18 October 1964. A 'Q' class 0-6-0 envelops the rear coaches with its exhaust.
Brian Stephenson

Left:
'Black Five' No 45288 passes Arundel with a Tring to Littlehampton excursion on 14 June 1957. The locomotive worked through from Tring.
E. W. Wilmshurst

Below:
Class N 2-6-0 No 31814 hauls 15 loaded hoppers and a brake on the 5am ballast train working from Salisbury to Three Bridges. The train is near Horsham on 6 June 1959. *J. Scrace*

Atlantics

The Brighton Atlantics were elegant engines as befitted a class often seen on the 'Southern Belle'. There were two series, 'H1' and 'H2', the latter surviving longer. In BR days they preserved the image of steam on the Brighton line with the Newhaven Continental service, but they did other work as well as seen in the following illustrations.

Above:
The 'H2' Atlantics are sometimes considered the better-looking because of the smooth line of the running plate from cylinders to firebox. In the 'H1' series the running plate undulated twice, once to clear the cylinders and then over the driving wheels. 'H2' No 2421 *South Foreland* **is at Newhaven on 4 September 1947 after working the down boat train from Victoria.** *C. C. B. Herbert*

Below:
Pictured at New Cross Gate on 1 September 1946 in wartime black livery, 'H1' Atlantic No 2038 was awaiting a duty that would take it to Brighton via Oxted and Uckfield. This locomotive was historically important as it was the locomotive that hauled, on 15 January 1945, the first Victoria-Newhaven boat train after its wartime cancellation. The locomotive was also, in 1947, the only 'H1' to be painted malachite green. *R. C. Riley*

Above left:
South Foreland gets under way from Bournemouth Central with the through train to Brighton in 1953. *D. E. Hodder*

Below left:
No 32424 **Beachy Head** has worked a private special from Victoria to Crowborough and is near South Malling on 21 August 1955 while returning to Lewes. The leading vehicle is an ex-SECR invalid saloon. Single-line working is in force during an engineers' possession. *S. C. Nash*

Above:
For comparison with Class H2, this picture of Class H1 No 2039 shows the broken line of the running plate. *IAL*

Right:
Commuters from the Sussex borders in the 1950s often rode home behind Brighton Atlantics on the 5.40pm from London Bridge to East Grinstead, here seen leaving the terminus in the charge of 'H2' Atlantic No 32426 **St Alban's Head** on 25 June 1952. *Brian Morrison*

Below right:
The Brighton via Oxted train is pictured approaching Clapham Junction behind No 2425 **Trevose Head** on 1 June 1950 conveying a rear portion for Tunbridge Wells West which will be detached at East Croydon. *C. C. B. Herbert*

Left:
No 32425 leaves Newhaven with the 4.30pm boat train on 22 June 1951. *Sidney Teasdale*

Above:
Smoke and steam are much in evidence as No 2426 *St Alban's Head* bustles through Newhaven Harbour station with an up relief boat train to Victoria. *D. A. West*

Right:
No 32421 *South Foreland* heads the 5.30pm parcels train to London Bridge out of Brighton on 4 July 1951. *P. Lynch*

Above:
On the eve of Nationalisation 'H1' Atlantic No 2039
Hartland Point was rebuilt at Brighton works to test the
sleeve valves for Bulleid's experimental 'Leader' class
locomotive. Transformed in a manner that gave no hint of
former elegance, *Hartland Point* ran trials between Brighton
and St Leonards or Groombridge. *IAL*

Below:
No 32424 was the last Brighton Atlantic and was in steam
for the last time on 13 April 1958 when it worked a Railway
Correspondence & Travel Society special to Newhaven and
then on to Brighton. Here it is backing into Brighton shed at
the end of its duty. It is unfortunate that none of the
Atlantics were to survive into preservation. *A. R. Butcher*

Main and Coast Lines

On the main line from Victoria and the coast lines east and west of Brighton certain services remained steam-worked until diesel traction took over.

Above:
'West Country' Pacific No 34098 *Templecombe* heads the through train to Bournemouth out of Brighton. *J. Davenport*

Below:
Ex-LBSCR 'K' class 2-6-0 No 32337 waits at Hove with a westbound freight on 26 September 1961. *D. H. Sawyer*

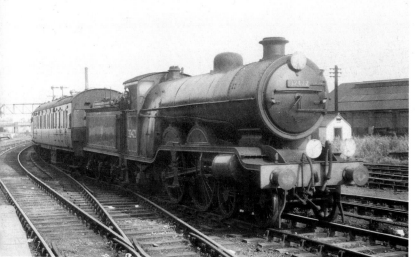

Above:
A Western Region excursion from Henley-on-Thames to Worthing and Littlehampton crosses the River Adur at Shoreham-by-Sea on August 21 1960. The locomotive is 'Battle of Britain' Pacific No 34066 *Spitfire.* S. Creer

Left:
A through train from Walsall to Hastings passes Latchmere Junction (West London Line) headed by 'H2' Atlantic No 32425 *Trevose Head* **on 30 June 1956.**
S. Creer

Below left:
No 32422 *North Foreland* **comes off the West London line at Willesden Junction on 1 August 1953 with a Summer Saturdays Only Hastings to Birmingham working.** C. R. L. Coles

Above right:
Ivatt 2-6-2T No 41302 heads the Birkenhead-Eastbourne train near Lewes on 14 July 1953. L. Elsey

Right:
'H2' Atlantic No 32424 — the last British Atlantic in traffic — is photographed at North Pole Junction, West London Line, on 31 August 1957 with the 12.35pm from Leicester to Hastings.
R. C. Riley

Left:
Standard '5MT' 4-6-0 No 73088, on an Eastbourne-Manchester train on 8 August 1964, passes sidings adjacent to Redhill MPD where 'N' 2-6-0 No 31827 and 'Q' 0-6-0 No 30531 await removal for scrapping. *G. D. King*

Below:
A Wood Street-Bognor excursion at Salfords on 30 August 1958 brings 'B1' 4-6-0 No 61249 *Fitzherbert Wright* on to Southern metals. *J. Scrace*

Left:
The Hastings-Leicester through train passes the site for the Hastings diesel depot soon after leaving St Leonards West Marina on 1 September 1956. The locomotive is 'N' class 2-6-0 No 31874. *D. Trevor Rowe*

Above:
'N' class 2-6-0 No 31827 approaches the Quarry Line tunnel at Redhill with a through train from the South Coast to the Midlands in August 1962. *G. D. King*

Below:
'U1' 2-6-0 No 31900 passes Brapool with the 6.34pm return excursion from Brighton to Chingford on 20 June 1964. The first eight coaches are ex-Great Eastern. *J. T. W. Kent*

Top:
'U1' 2-6-0 No 31899 leaves Quarry Tunnel on 1 June 1957 with an excursion from Kettering to Brighton. *S. Creer*

Above:
The up boat train from Newhaven Harbour approaches Lewes East Sidings on 20 April 1952, headed by 'Schools' No 30922 *Marlborough*. *S. C. Nash*

Top:
'Schools' No 30924 *Haileybury* with the coaches from
Hastings waits at Redhill on 28 October 1961 for the
portions from Margate and Ramsgate to be attached,
forming a through train from Sussex and Kent to
Wolverhampton. *R. N. Joanes*

Above:
Fairburn 2-6-4T No 42104 approaches Lewes on 21 August
1955 with a Newhaven-Redhill coal special. *S. C. Nash*

47

Left:
'H15' 4-6-0 No 30332 arrives in Chichester reception yard from Salisbury on 10 March 1956.
C. R. L. Coles

Below left:
In the final days of steam 'Schools' No 30917 *Ardingly* **leaves Brighton on the through train to Plymouth, passing 'K' class 2-6-0 No 32343.**
Brian Haresnape

Above right:
A Class L1 4-4-0, No 31783, is caught east of Polegate with a Hertford North-Hastings excursion on 15 August 1954. *S. C. Nash*

Right:
Class K No 2345 leaves London Bridge with vans for Bognor on 21 March 1949. *Pamlin Prints*

Below:
Class K 2-6-0 No 32348 heads a through train from Eastbourne to Leicester via Brighton on Falmer Bank on 19 July 1958.
W. M. J. Jackson

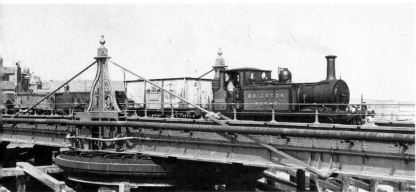

Above:
The 'Terrier' *Brighton Works* **has collected wagons in the West Goods Yard at Newhaven and approaches the exit on to the main road over the swing bridge.**
A. R. Butcher

Left:
The 'Terrier' crosses the swing bridge over the River Ouse on the 'tramway' track at the side of the road *A. R. Butcher*

Below left:
Class A1X No 32636, allocated to Brighton, crosses the swing bridge at Newhaven on 12 July 1950.
R. C. Riley

Right:
Class A1X 'Terrier' 0-6-0T No 32678 leaves Seaford for Newhaven with a special van train.
S. C. Nash

Selected Shed Allocations

Ashford (74A) as at 1959

Class Z	30951, 30952
Class H	31005, 31263, 31276, 31307, 31319, 31519, 31520, 31522
Class C	31218, 31219, 31221, 31223, 31589
Class D1	31246, 31727
Class N	31400, 31401, 31402, 31403, 31404, 31405, 31406, 31407, 31848, 31854
Class L1	31756, 31757, 31758, 31759, 31782
Class A1X	32636
Class 4 (Fairburn)	42096, 42097, 42098, 42099, 42100
Class 2 (BR)	84020, 84021, 84022, 84023, 84024

Dover (74C) as at 1959

Class 57xx	4601, 4610, 4616, 4626, 4630, 4631
Class B4	30084
'King Arthur'	30775 *Air Agravaine*, 30777 *Sir Lamiel*, 30797 *Sir Blamor de Ganis*, 30798 *Sir Hectimere*, 30804 *Sir Cador of Cornwall*, 30805 *Sir Constantine*
Class R1	31010, 31047, 31107, 31128, 31174, 31337
Class P	31027, 31323
Class O1	31065, 31258, 31425, 31430, 31434
Class C	31113, 31150, 31191, 31243
Class H	31328, 31542
Class L1	31753, 31754, 31755, 31788, 31789
Class N	31818, 31819, 31820, 31821
'Battle of Britain'	34070 *Manston*, 34071 *249 Squadron*, 34082 *615 Squadron*, 34083 *605 Squadron*, 34084 *253 Squadron*
'West Country'	34103 *Calstock*
Class 4 (Fairburn)	42074, 42075, 42076, 42077, 42078, 42079, 42092, 42095
Class 4 (BR)	75065, 75066, 75067, 75068, 75069

Tonbridge (74D) as at 1959

Class H	31164, 31177, 31193, 31239, 31259, 31266, 31279, 31295, 31517, 31523, 31543
Class C	31244, 31270, 31272, 31280, 31588, 31590, 31716
Class D1	31470, 31487, 31489, 31492
Class L	31760, 31762, 31763, 31770, 31771, 31773
Class U1	31896, 31908, 31909, 31910
Class E3	32456
Class E4	32578, 32580
Class Q1	33024, 33028, 33029, 33030, 33031, 33032, 33033, 33034, 33035, 33036

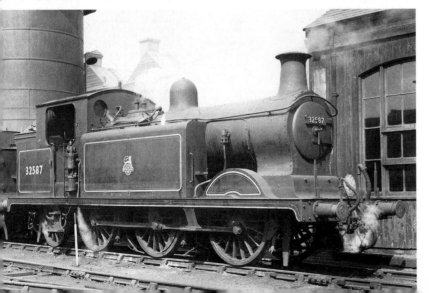

Above:
A 'Schools' on the Newhaven boat train. No 30912 *Downside* passes Balham with the down service on 16 June 1956. *S. Creer*

Left:
'U1' class 2-6-0 No 31899 passes through Lewes station with the down Newhaven Continental in August 1952. *A. A. Sellman*

Below left:
'E5' 0-6-2T No 32587 at Brighton in BR livery. *LGRP*

'Cuckoo Line' Services

The line from Eridge to Polegate via Heathfield provided a reasonably direct route from the Tonbridge/Tunbridge Wells area to Eastbourne.

It was called the 'Cuckoo Line' because of the tradition that the first Cuckoo of the summer was heard on the day of Heathfield Fair.

Above:
Standard 2-6-4T No 80011 leaves Eastbourne with the 6pm to Tonbridge on 2 September 1964. *G. D. King*

Below:
No 80011 leaves Hailsham with the 4.35pm Tunbridge Wells West-Eastbourne service. This train also conveyed through coaches off the 3.52pm from Victoria. *S. C. Nash*

Left:
Departure from Eastbourne by the 10.45am service to Tunbridge Wells West on 19 April 1962 with Standard 2-6-4T No 80095 emitting an impressive exhaust.
P. J. Lynch

Left:
Class H 0-4-4T No 31164 works hard to lift the 1.53pm Tunbridge Wells West-Eastbourne train up Rotherfield bank on 18 June 1955.
S. C. Nash

Below:
A week later No 31310 tackles the bank in more sedate fashion on the same service. *S. C. Nash*

Top:
On 3 June 1962 the 10.45am service from Eastbourne to Tunbridge Wells is seen departing from Mayfield behind Class H 0-4-4T No 31518. The ex-LBSCR line from Eridge to Polegate was to lose its passenger services in two stages during the 1960s: on 14 June 1965 the section between Eridge (Redgate Mill Junction) and Hailsham closed, whilst the southern section from Hailsham to Polegate succumbed on 9 September 1968. *S. C. Nash*

Above:
Standard 2-6-4T No 80018 is near Polegate on the 'Cuckoo Line' with the 4.39pm from Eastbourne to Tunbridge Wells West. *E. R. Wethersett*

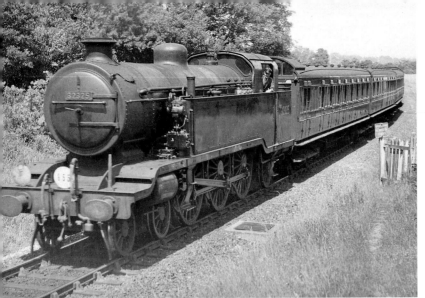

Left:
Ex-LBSC Class J1 4-6-2T No 32325 heads the 11.8am Victoria-Eastbourne via Hailsham service on 30 June 1950. *E. R. Wethersett*

Left:
BR Standard Class 4 2-6-4T No 80017 approaches Groombridge with the 2.45pm Eastbourne-Tunbridge Wells West service on 15 April 1961. *Dennis C. Ovenden*

Below:
Horam station on the 'Cuckoo Line' is pictured on 28 May 1965, with 2-6-4T No 80072 on the 3.14pm departure from Tunbridge Wells West to Eastbourne. *Stephen Talligs*

SER to Hastings

The South Eastern's efforts to penetrate Sussex were rewarded in 1845 when the company was authorised to extend its Tunbridge Wells branch to Hastings. Main line steam services between Charing Cross and Hastings by this route continued until 1958 when the Hastings diesels finally took over.

Above:
'Britannia' class Pacific No 70004 *William Shakespeare* is pictured with steam to spare on Hildenborough Bank with the down 'Golden Arrow' on 23 May 1953. Representatives of the first BR Standard class were to be based at Stewarts Lane for a period for working this prestige train. *Brian Morrison*

Below:
Also photographed on 23 May 1953 at Hildenborough was 'C' class 0-6-0 No 31229 hauling the 3.16pm local service from Tunbridge Wells to Sevenoaks tender first. Note the superb pre-Grouping coaching stock. *Brian Morrison*

Left:
A 'Schools' is caught entering Hastings station in June 1951; No 30904 *Lancing. A. A. Sellman*

Below left:
The 2.10pm Sundays Hastings-Charing Cross service approaches Tonbridge on 14 February 1955 double-headed by 'L' class 4-4-0 No 31773 and 'Schools' No 30900 *Eton. B. C. Bending*

Above:
'Schools' class 4-4-0 No 30901 *Winchester* **arrives at Crowhurst with a Charing Cross-Hastings train.** *A. A. Sellman*

Right:
On shed at Tonbridge (74D) on 26 March 1953 was Class D 4-4-0 No 31728. *Brian Morrison*

Below right:
Seven years later, three Class H 0-4-4Ts, Nos 31522, 31500 and 31193, were present at Tonbridge shed. By this date the shed had been recoded 73J. In June 1962 it became a sub-shed of Stewarts Lane until the latter closed in September 1963. It then became a sub-shed to Redhill until closure in January 1965. *D. M. C. Hepburne-Scott/Rail Archive Stephenson*

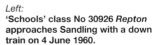

Above:
En route for Bexhill West on 11 August 1955, 'H' class No 31162 propels its two-coach push-pull set. *E. C. Griffith*

Below:
Another 'H' class 0-4-4T, No 31279, with the 10.15am departure from Crowhurst to Bexhill West, leaves Crowhurst on 9 August 1953. *E. C. Griffith*

Right:
With Bo-Peep Tunnel closed in April 1950, Charing Cross-Hastings trains were diverted to Bexhill. 'Schools' class No 30901 *Winchester* arrives at Crowhurst with a Bexhill-Charing Cross train. The locomotive of the push-pull set which maintained a connection with St Leonards is seen in the background. *G. H. Bell*

Centre right:
Robertsbridge was the junction for the Kent & East Sussex Railway. A Robertsbridge-Northiam 'Hop-pickers Friends' excursion on September 20 1953 is worked by two 'Terriers' — No 32326 leading, banked in the rear by No 32658. *S. C. Nash*

Below:
'Schools' class 4-4-0 No 30903 *Charterhouse* is seen at Robertsbridge on 26 September 1953 with a main line service. *R. C. Riley*

KENT

Elated after his first journey from Paris to the Channel coast over the TGV Nord, President Mitterand of France is reported to have suggested that travel at the British end of the Tunnel would give passengers time to admire the scenery but little to boast about in the matter of speed. Sniping at British Rail has become commonplace but rarely from so distinguished a source.

There was a time when the ride through Kent to a Channel port was an enjoyable prelude to a holiday on the Continent. The anxieties of getting baggage registered at Victoria were over and the unfamiliar travel tickets had been proved to work at the barrier. Now was the time to relax and enjoy the panorama of the Kent countryside before steeling oneself for the shuffle, laden with suitcases, through cavernous quayside sheds to the ship under the impassive gaze of Customs and Immigration officers and Police.

Changes of route to and from the ports added interest and a spice of variety to the journey. Looking out for a landmark such as Tonbridge, the passenger might find that he was passing Maidstone instead. Closer to London the possibilities were wider. Somebody with a taste for curious facts once calculated that the Southern could reach its Eastern Section London termini from Tonbridge by 41 different routes. It is a remarkable fact that when the great landslide occurred at Folkestone Warren on 19 December 1915 the vital wartime traffic to the port of Dover was not interrupted and continued to use alternative routes until after the end of the war. The line between Folkestone and Dover was reopened on 11 August 1919.

The variety of routes reflects the railway history of Kent. First in the field outside the London area was the Canterbury & Whitstable Railway, a somewhat under-publicised undertaking which actually began operations with a steam locomotive on 3 May 1830, over four months before the Liverpool & Manchester. However, the locomotive *Invicta* soon quailed before the steep gradients out of Whitstable and was confined to working on a level section of the line 1 mile 330yd long.

The first railway to Dover was the South Eastern whose line from Reigate (now Redhill) to

Below:
A train from Dover via Ashford is brought into London Bridge by 'Schools' No 30929 *Malvern. D. Sellman*

63

the port via Ashford was opened as far as Folkestone on 28 June 1843. South Eastern trains shared the route from London Bridge to Reigate with the London, Brighton & South Coast Railway. Eastwards from Reigate to Ashford was the celebrated stretch of 46 miles almost dead straight and level.

In 1843 the company had bought Folkestone Harbour and built the harbour branch to serve it but this was used only for freight for five years. After an inspection by the Board of Trade it was passed for passenger traffic at the end of 1848. Meanwhile, after extensive tunnelling between Folkestone and Dover, and the blowing up of part of Round Down cliff, the line was opened throughout on 7 February 1844.

The Reigate-Tonbridge section was bypassed when the direct line from New Cross to Tonbridge was opened in 1868. This became the main line and down trains were faced with an almost unbroken climb at 1 in 120-140 for 11¾ miles to the summit at Knockholt. Up trains had to face the Hildenborough bank of six miles mainly at 1 in 122, beginning after the slack to 40mph at Tonbridge where the new line curved sharply away from the old route via Redhill.

Secure, as it thought, in possession of the 19th century equivalent of the traditional Dover Road, the South Eastern was not at first perturbed by the activities of the East Kent Railway. This company had opened a line between Strood and Canterbury on 9 June 1860. It then obtained powers to extend to Dover, where it arrived in 1861. The climate of tolerance changed when the East Kent was authorised to enter London and the first plans were strenuously opposed by the South Eastern. The East Kent tried again, this time pointing out that existing lines in Kent were acknowledged to be working to capacity, and that London Bridge was not a convenient terminus for the West End. Victoria station was under construction and access lines were being built. Eventually the East Kent was authorised to send its trains into Victoria by running powers over the West End of London & Crystal Palace and the Victoria Station & Pimlico Railways. The route was via Crystal Palace, Balham and Wandsworth (later renamed Clapham and then Clapham Junction). The Crystal Palace line was sold to the LBSCR in 1859 but the Victoria Station & Pimlico survived as a company until the Southern Railway was formed.

On gaining access to London the East Kent changed its name to the London Chatham & Dover Railway. The name was not fully descriptive for a second main line branching from the Dover line at Faversham served a string of resorts along the North Kent coast to Ramsgate, Broadstairs and Margate.

Sharing tracks from Crystal Palace into London with the Brighton company's trains was unsatisfactory and in 1863 the LC&D opened a new line from Penge Junction which by-passed most of the former route, not rejoining it until Stewarts Lane Junction, Battersea. In later years a new line was built which avoided Stewarts Lane Junction, crossed over the South Western lines on a viaduct near Queens Road station and gave independent entry to the Chatham side of Victoria.

Many will remember Queens Road Battersea (now Queenstown Road) as a unique spotters' vantage point, commanding both the Waterloo traffic and the trains to and from Victoria on their viaduct beyond the station, together with a glimpse of locomotive movements to and from Stewarts Lane depot on a lower level. South Eastern and London, Chatham & Dover interests often clashed in Kent but by the end of the century both companies had realised that conflict was of no benefit to either. On 1 January 1899 the management of both systems was vested in a South Eastern & Chatham Joint Committee. From then until Grouping the rail network in Kent became the South Eastern & Chatham Railway. On the eve of its absorption into the Southern Railway the Chairman, Mr Cosmo Bonsor, recalled the inauspicious omens of the early years of the Joint Committee in words that have a familiar ring: 'I do not think I am exaggerating when I say that when the South Eastern and the Chatham companies came together they were both singularly unpopular. Their services were bad. The complaints, both public and private, as to the unpunctuality of their trains were very numerous, and I think I might almost add that they were a standing joke with the clown of the pantomime and with the comic gentlemen in the music halls.'

Even in the 1960s survivors of the South Eastern locomotive stock were to be seen. Reminders of the London, Chatham & Dover had mostly gone but stories are still told of the days when its boat trains raced those of the South Eastern to be first at Admiralty Pier, Dover. A daily paper of the period commented on 'a new form of gambling among idlers on the pier' who laid bets as to which train would be first past the post: 'when the signals have fallen on both tracks the excitement becomes intense. The SER has a clear run in by the shore and when the train shoots out of the tunnel the backers of Charing Cross are jubilant: but, as often as not, Victoria suddenly shoots round the corner and wins, like a well-ridden thoroughbred, by a short head.'

In their book *Express Trains, English and Foreign* (1889) E. Foxwell and T. C. Farrer were critical of the punctuality of the southern lines (although showing more understanding of their problems than Network SouthEast receives today). They had a soft spot for the London, Chatham & Dover which they described as 'our youngest, poorest and pluckiest line'. It was also far-sighted. Its City branch from Herne Hill to Blackfriars, later extended to join the Metropolitan at Farringdon Street on 1 January 1866, was a forerunner of Thameslink.

The Chatham company was anxious that its City extension should not be seen simply as a means of transporting workers in the Square Mile between the suburbs and their offices. Travellers were reminded that the connection at Herne Hill with the rest of the system offered wider possibilities. To this end the station frontage at Blackfriars was decorated with 54 tiles carrying the names of interesting destinations at home and abroad. Kent coast resorts naturally figure in the display, but Rome and Florence beckoned the romantic traveller, while St Petersburg challenged the adventurous. The tiles were preserved in the concourse of the rebuilt Blackfriars station.

Detective fiction has also accorded the railway a permanent memorial. When Sherlock Holmes and Dr Watson sought refuge on the Continent to elude pursuit by Professor Moriarty, the 'Napoleon of crime', they took the Dover train at Victoria. The Professor, hard on their heels, was left fuming on the platform but the Chatham company produced a special for him in record time. Holmes and Watson gave their pursuer the slip by alighting at Canterbury. 'Already, you see,' said Holmes, pointing up the line where 'far away from among the Kentish woods there arose a thin spray of smoke'. There was barely time to hide behind a pile of luggage before the special, consisting of an engine and one carriage, roared through the station, swayed and rocked over the points and was gone.

From Canterbury Holmes and Watson continued their journey by an unspecified route to Newhaven and crossed to Dieppe, reaching Brussels the same night. Cross-country journeys on both sides of the Channel must have been faster in those days.

By the time of the railway modernisation plan in 1955 electrification in Kent had reached Gillingham, Maidstone and Sevenoaks but the longer-distance services to the Channel ports and the Kent coast were still worked by steam. The modernisation plan, however, gave priority to extending electrification to the coast, first from Gillingham to Ramsgate, including the Sheerness branch, and from Faversham to Dover. This was Phase 1 of the project, inaugurated in 1959. Phase 2 covered most of the remaining lines, including Sevenoaks to Dover via Tonbridge and Ashford and came into operation in 1962.

There were still reminders of the South Eastern in the last days of steam. James Stirling, when Locomotive Superintendent of the company, had introduced the 'R' class 0-6-0T. They were rebuilt later with domed boilers and became Class R1, surviving into the late 1950s. Three with shorter chimneys and cut-down cabs for working on the old Canterbury & Whitstable line were still active elsewhere in 1957. The modification was necessary for working through Tyler Hill Tunnel, Canterbury. The bore was only 12ft high and until 1846 trains were worked through it with cable haulage by the Tyler Hill winding engine. The Southern Railway withdrew passenger services in 1931 but freight traffic continued under British Railways until 1952. There was an unwelcome reminder of the presence of the tunnel in 1974 when part of it collapsed, causing damage by subsidence to a building of the University of Kent.

H. S. Wainwright succeeded James Stirling as Locomotive Superintendent of the South Eastern Railway in 1898 and was in office at the time of the merger. His first locomotives were the long-lived Class C 0-6-0s which were still in service at the time of the Kent coast electrification Phase 2 in 1962, albeit in somewhat faded form. Wainwright originally adopted a bright green livery with polished brass dome covers and copper caps to the chimneys, perhaps symbolising a new broom in the shape of the Joint Committee. The survivors in the 1960s showed no sign of their former glory. His first 4-4-0 express locomotive was Class D in 1901. It was a handsome locomotive and in its green paint and polished brass became a popular subject for railway jigsaw puzzles and colour plates in magazines. The class had 6ft 8in driving wheels, 19in by 26in cylinders and 175lb boiler pressure. In their last days on British Railways they still preserved the Wainwright image although in less colourful form and on less prestigious trains. Stopping services on the Tonbridge-Reading line were among their last duties.

Wainwright introduced two more passenger 4-4-0 classes. In Class E the driving wheels were reduced in diameter to 6ft 6in and all had Belpaire fireboxes. A number were rebuilt with larger boilers, superheaters and piston valves, forming Class E1. Seven of the E1 class were still at work on British Rail in the late 1950s. A more enduring class was Wainwright's Class L which went into service in 1914 after his retirement. By that time bridge strengthening had allowed the permissible axle load to be increased from 18 tons to 19¼ tons and Wainwright took advantage of this to produce a large 4-4-0 express passenger locomotive with 6ft 8in wheels, cylinders 20½in by 26in, and 160lb boiler pressure. All were superheated.

A hardy survivor of the Wainwright years was his Class H 0-4-4T, a versatile design working local passenger and freight services and sometimes to be seen piloting larger locomotives.

R. E. L. Maunsell succeeded Wainwright as Locomotive Superintendent in 1913. During the years of World War 1 he introduced his highly successful Moguls of Classes N and N1. Both had large taper boilers carrying 200lb pressure, superheaters and 5ft 6in wheels. Class N had two 19in by 28in cylinders. Class N1 had three 16in by 28in cylinders. All were familiar in the 1960s. Maunsell's last design for the SECR was a 2-6-4 passenger tank engine. This was intended for the Kent Coast expresses of the future and was in the tradition of the express passenger tank engine as seen on the LBSCR in the 4-6-2 and 4-6-4 Classes J and L. More of Maunsell's engines were built after Grouping and were given 'River' names. On 24 August 1927 No 800 *River Cray* was working the 5pm from Cannon Street to Folkestone when the leading wheels derailed between Dunton Green and Sevenoaks. A little further on, the trailing bogie also left the rails and on reaching a pair of trailing points the whole train derailed.

Unfortunately there was an overbridge at this point and coaches were crushed against the abutment. The casualty list was 13 killed and 21 seriously injured.

Detailed investigations and tests after the accident supported the view that surging of water in the side tanks, possibly set up by a slight irregularity in the track, made the engine unstable. All the 'Rivers' were rebuilt as 2-6-0 tender engines, forming the nucleus of Class U, of which more were built by the Southern Railway. These were two-cylinder engines. One of the 'Rivers' which had been built with three cylinders was rebuilt as a 2-6-0 and others followed to form the three-cylinder 'U1' class.

In the 1950s excellent work was still being done by Maunsell's rebuild of Wainwright's 'L' class 4-4-0, converting it to Class L1. The changes included raising the boiler pressure, increasing the valve travel, using smaller cylinders and improving the draughting. The immediate requirement was to provide power for the restoration in 1926 of the 80min timings between Charing Cross and Folkestone with heavier rolling stock and one intermediate stop. The new locomotives could handle loads of 320 tons on this schedule compared with the maximum of 225 tons on a non-stop run with Class L. The 'L1s' soon found a much wider field of application.

Outside southeast England the image of the railways in Kent tended to be dominated by the boat trains. The southwest and the West Country were the favoured holiday destinations in many parts of the country but the Kent coast holiday resorts from Herne Bay to Deal attracted holidaymakers from the London area in their thousands. They also drew holidaymakers from the Midlands and North. Up to World War 2 through restaurant car trains had run at weekends between Birmingham and the Kent coast with through coaches from Manchester and Liverpool.

The traffic continued in BR days. It has been recorded that 66 Kent coast trains ran on 26 July 1958 and despite the availability at that time of Bulleid's light Pacifics, earlier classes predominated, some of them with SECR origins. The 2-6-0s were the most numerous totalling 12 'N' class and 15 'U1'. There were 20 4-4-0s (15 'Schools' one 'L' class, one 'E1' and three 'D1s'). The 4-6-0s totalled 13 (six 'King Arthurs', five BR Standard Class 5 and two BR Standard Class 4). Six light Pacifics made up the total. Electrification and diesel power have 'flattened' the gradients which challenged the steam locomotives and their crews. Less well-known than Shap or Dainton but still formidable was Sole Street bank which faced up trains on the Chatham line. Approached by a severe slack round the Rochester curve, the gradient was almost unbroken at 1 in 100 for five miles to Sole Street station.

Folkestone, Dover and Deal did not generate traffic from Charing Cross to quite the same extent. A feature of the working on that section was the operation, partly for stock movements, of 'roundabout' trains which ran outwards from Charing Cross to Folkestone, Dover and Deal, returning via Ramsgate and Margate to Victoria. The direct line from Dover to Deal was a joint undertaking by the LCDR and the SER, opened in 1881. Previously Deal had been served by a branch from Minster on the South Eastern's line from Canterbury to Margate and Ramsgate.

At summer weekends some holiday trains started from outer London stations. Departures for the coast from Blackheath or Gravesend, for example, travelled via Strood and needed a banker from Strood up to the main line. This work might be entrusted to a Wainwright 'O1' 0-6-0 (his rebuild of Stirling's Class O) or his still numerous Class C of the same wheel arrangement. Towards the end of steam a diesel shunter might be used. One observer at Tonbridge has noted a through train from Sevenoaks to Tonbridge which 'more often than not would trundle into Tonbridge behind one of the Southern's sturdy little 'C' class 0-6-0s'. Among hardy survivors into the electric period there is also a record of an ex-SECR 'D1' 4-4-0 which used to work empty stock from Stewarts Lane to Blackfriars where it reversed and propelled the coaches into Cannon Street in readiness to depart with its train as the 5.22pm to Dover.

Connections between the South Eastern and London, Chatham & Dover routes to the coast near Chislehurst had been made in 1902-04, soon after the amalgamation. After Grouping they enabled the Southern Railway to concentrate all its boat train services at Victoria but they also affected services between London and the Kent coast. As the popularity of commuting between seaside towns and London grew, long-distance commuter trains could take passengers from the North Kent coastal 'dormitories' to London Bridge and Cannon Street for easy access to city offices.

As early as 1921 the SECR had decided that the Kent coast traffic justified running a Sundays only all-Pullman express between Victoria and Ramsgate. It was named the 'Thanet Pullman Limited' and ran non-stop over the 74 miles from Victoria to Margate in 90min before calling at Broadstairs and terminating at Ramsgate. The Southern Railway continued the service, but patronage of the Pullmans was small and ordinary coaches were substituted, at length only one Pullman remaining in the formation. After World War 2 an all-Pullman train to the Kent coast was revived in 1948 and named 'Thanet Belle' to conform with the Region's other 'Belle' Pullman services. It ran daily in the summer, serving Whitstable, Herne Bay, Margate, Broadstairs and Ramsgate and was formed of two first class and eight second (ie standard) class Pullmans. In the winter a train of ordinary stock with two Pullmans was substituted. In the summer of 1949 the all-Pullman 'Belle', reappeared and on Saturdays made two round trips. Two years later the non-stop run to Whitstable was interrupted by a stop at Faversham to detach two through cars for Canterbury and the name of the train was changed to 'Kentish Belle'. This facility was withdrawn in 1952 and non-stop running between Victoria and Whitstable was restored. The 'Kentish Belle', ceased to exist when Phase 1 of the Kent coast electrification was inaugurated.

The main line from Charing Cross via Tonbridge and Ashford also had its named train. The 'Man of Kent', introduced in 1953, revived an 80min timing from Charing Cross to Folkestone Central with one stop that had operated for some years between the wars. The train was once a preserve of the 'Schools' 4-4-0s but earlier the same schedule with a stop at Waterloo Junction (now Waterloo East) had been entrusted to Maunsell's 'L1' rebuilds of Wainwright's 'L' class. The train was restored in 1953, retaining its original time of 4.15pm from Charing Cross and 5.35pm arrival at Folkestone but now it was named 'Man of Kent'. The return working of the stock was at 10.14am from Sandwich. This service, also, was named 'Man of Kent' and had the 80min timing from Folkestone to Charing Cross. With loads of 350 tons and more the 'Schools' had to work hard, especially on the long climbs in both directions to Knockholt Summit. Over the straight and level stretch between Tonbridge and Ashford, speeds of 80mph and more were common. When

electrification took over in 1961 there was a train from Charing Cross to Folkestone at 4pm which made the journey with one stop in 78min, but it was now one of a series of hourly trains and was unnamed.

In the Grouping years the boat trains serving the Short Sea Routes to the Continent were increasing in weight and Maunsell's 'Lord Nelson' class locomotives were designed specifically for these duties. They were very much a part of the railway scene in Kent until the boat trains were withdrawn on the outbreak of World War 2. By the time they were restored after the war, Bulleid's light Pacifics were available and the 'Nelsons' left the Stewarts Lane depot with which they had been so long associated.

For many years the morning 'Continental' service had left London at 11am. In 1929 it was decided to run an all-Pullman train for first class passengers only to Dover, where it would connect with a cross-Channel ship, the *Canterbury*, built specially for the service. At Calais the Northern Railway of France provided a connecting Pullman express to Paris, the Flèche d'Or. For some years before the war the return Channel crossing was from Boulogne to Folkestone. The Folkestone Harbour branch had been built originally for freight traffic and with 1 in 30 for ¾ mile boasted the steepest gradient on the Southern system. In later years it was the scene of one of those endearing railway oddities. Boat trains were laboriously heaved up to Folkestone Junction by three or sometimes

four tank engines where the train engine was waiting to back on and continue the journey to London. The operation involved a change of direction which was perplexing to passengers who had chosen a seat as they thought 'facing engine'. On the down journey progress was cautious in the extreme. Passengers in a 'crack' train in those days felt a sense of superiority and it was an irritation that pedestrians plodding up on the adjacent road hardly bothered to turn their heads.

The up 'Golden Arrow' in its early days had a fast timing. The 'Nelson' which was the normal power had to run the first 41.4 miles to passing Tonbridge in 42.5min. The 35 miles from Sandling Junction to Tonbridge were allowed 33min only, a scheduled average of 65.3mph. The timing onwards was easier to allow for the stiff climb to Knockholt and cautious running through the London suburbs.

Soon after it was introduced in 1929 the depression years of the 1930s and the growing popularity of air travel among the clientele which had been targeted made it necessary to abandon the all-Pullman image. The service was withdrawn on the outbreak of war but restored, again as all-Pullman, on 15 April 1946. The formation was then 10 Pullmans and two vans and the locomotive was a 'Merchant Navy' or a 'West Country' Pacific, or in later years a BR Standard 'Britannia' Pacific. Large gilt arrows on the smokebox door and on the sides added panache but could not arrest another decline in Pullman patronage. Eventually there were only four first class Pullmans, the other vehicles being ordinary second (standard) class coaches. After the second phase of Kent coast electrification a Class 71 electric locomotive took over the working. The train was withdrawn at the end of the summer service of 1972.

Early morning travellers at suburban stations on the lines into Victoria got to know the blue Wagons-Lits cars of the 'Night Ferry' although its time tended to be unpredictable. The 'Night Ferry' service of through sleeping cars between London and Paris via the Dover-Dunkerque train ferry began in 1936. The train followed the Chatham route between London and Dover. During the prewar years it was double-headed by 'L1' or 'L' class 4-4-0s. When the service was resumed in 1947 Bulleid's light Pacifics took charge but increasing loads still required a pilot, usually a 4-4-0. In the later years of steam 'Merchant Navy' or 'Britannia' BR Standard Pacifics were allotted to the train.

The service was popular with businessmen who appreciated arriving in Paris after a night's sleep and breakfast on the train from Dunkerque, putting them in good form for early appointments. Even enthusiasts for air travel were to be seen on board in winter when aircraft might be subject to delays and diversions, possibly landing them miles from where they wanted to be. This advantage of the train was slowly eroded by improvements in aircraft blind landing systems and soon the cost of renewing the ageing stock tipped the economic balance. After the first phase of the Kent coast electrification the 'Night Ferry' continued with electric or electro-diesel haulage but made its last run on 31 October 1980.

At times of heavy traffic the departure of boat trains from the ports was liable to be delayed by Customs examination of passengers' luggage. Alternative paths were available, taking advantage of the variety of routes the Southern had inherited from its forebears in Kent. Passengers unfamiliar with the railway geography of the county were often surprised to find themselves passing Maidstone when they had been looking out for Tonbridge. The line from Ashford to Maidstone was a legacy of the London, Chatham & Dover. It had been bitterly opposed by the South Eastern but with its continuation from Maidstone via Otford to Swanley it later became a useful diversionary route for belated boat trains.

Perhaps unjustly, the area bordering the Thames and Medway estuaries is often seen as bleak and unfriendly. The Southern Railway shrugged off these prejudices in 1932 by building a branch 1¾ miles long from Stoke Junction on the Port Victoria line to Allhallows-on-Sea. A developer had hoped to promote this spot on the Thames estuary as a holiday resort. The project did not get beyond a caravan site and a hotel but in 1935 the railway thought it worth doubling the line. Through coaches from London and summer excursions were operated for a time but the resort did not flourish. The branch remained, however, until 4 December 1961 when passenger traffic was withdrawn. Latterly it was served by push-pull sets to and from Gravesend worked by 'H' class 0-4-4 tanks which had superseded ex-LCDR tanks of Class R.

Further east, the Isle of Sheppey was served by a branch from the LCDR at Sittingbourne opened on 19 June 1860. The line crossed the Swale on the Kings Ferry bridge which carried both the rail line and a roadway and replaced the ferry which had given Sheppey its 'island' status. A branch was opened to Queenborough Pier in 1876, causing friction with the South Eastern Railway which had taken over the Hundred of Hoo Railway connecting its Gravesend-Strood line with the opposite bank of the Medway at Port Victoria on the Isle of Grain. Both ports were used at different periods by shipping services to Flushing. Port Victoria was also a convenient spot for visiting foreign monarchs and their families to disembark without attracting large crowds of spectators. Today the old Port Victoria site has been taken over by a new container port and Freightliner terminal.

Up to the outbreak of World War 2 the Southern Railway ran a 'mini-boat train' to Gravesend West in connection with sailings to Rotterdam. It was formed of three or four coaches of boat train stock, complete with headboards and was usually hauled by a 'C' class 0-6-0 or an 'H' class 0-4-4T. Gravesend West station remained open until 1953, served only by two-coach push-pull sets but retaining some bilingual signposts as a reminder of its past.

The South Eastern Railway branch from Sandling Junction reached the coast at Sandgate via Hythe. There was no direct rail link between Sandgate and New Romney, terminus of a branch from Lydd on the Appledore-Dungeness line. In 1926 the gap of some 15 miles along the coast was filled by the 15in gauge Romney, Hythe & Dymchurch Railway. This is a replica in miniature of a steam-operated main line, its trains hauled by Pacific and 4-8-2 locomotives styled to reflect the main line express locomotives of the day. Throughout the 1930s the railway provided an appreciated transport service for local communities as well as being a tourist attraction. In World War 2 it found itself in a restricted area and was put to good account by providing armoured trains to patrol the coastal track.

Since the war, roads in the area have improved or better bus services have taken traffic which once went by rail but in the summer holiday season the line attracts tourists in large numbers. Once it appealed by being a main line in miniature. Today this appeal is reinforced by preserving the sights and sounds of engines in steam.

Several railways in Kent were built by Col H. F. Stephens under Light Railways orders. Two which survived to be taken over by British Railways were the East Kent Light Railways and the Kent & East Sussex Railway.

The East Kent system was planned to serve the Kent coalfield and some 19 miles of line were built from Shepherdswell on the SECR, between Canterbury and Dover, to Wingham Colliery. Most of the line was closed after the BR takeover but the short section from Shepherdswell to Tilmanstone Colliery remained open until the colliery closed.

The Kent & East Sussex Railway ran between the Tonbridge-Hastings line at Robertsbridge and the Tonbridge-Ashford-Dover line at Headcorn. At Grouping the line remained independent, continuing to provide a valuable service to the local communities in a largely agricultural environment. Its operations were not confined to the rails but a road motor collection and delivery service was also run. Passenger services were withdrawn in 1954 but goods traffic between Robertsbridge and Tenterden continued until 1961. Among the varied assortment of motive power acquired by Col Stephens was an ex-LBSC 'Terrier' which worked on the line with the name *Bodiam* until passenger trains were withdrawn. This engine was evidently a source of particular pride to the company. The late C. Hamilton Ellis reported in *The Railway Magazine* of May 1935 that the railway could boast of a locomotive that looked as locomotives used to look. He commented that the Stroudley Terrier No 3, formerly *Bodiam*, had been rebuilt and put into running order. 'She is painted a bright apple green, lined out with black and white, and lettered in yellow and black ... The copper capped chimney has been retained, and the top left bright.' Hamilton Ellis commented that 'a locomotive that is a thing of beauty is a rarity in these days of paint shop economy and little cleaning'. So much for the Golden Age we dream about!

The Boat Trains

For many people memories of steam in Kent are centred on journeys to the Channel Ports. At one time the mere act of taking his seat in a Continental boat train seemed to distance the traveller in a gratifying manner from those on adjacent platforms scurrying in and out of trains of a more mundane sort. Gradually, however, the boat train image faded, eroded first by the airlines and then by the car ferries. Travellers eccentric enough to have chosen the train were instructed peremptorily to separate themselves from the motorists before disembarking. At length the boat trains were patronised to a large extent by those whom British Rail classified as 'backpack traffic'. The following pages reflect a more glamorous past.

Below left:
The postwar 'Ferry': 'Merchant Navy' Pacific No 35029 *Ellerman Lines* **comes off the Petts Wood-Bickley loop at Bickley Junction on 11 August 1951 hauling the Victoria-bound 'Night Ferry' stock from Paris.** *Brian Morrison*

Below:
The down 'Golden Arrow' in BR days passes Petts Wood headed by 'Battle of Britain' unrebuilt Pacific No 34086 *219 Squadron.* *Derek Cross*

Left:
An up Continental train in the shadow of Shakespeare Cliff, Dover, leaves a towering exhaust plume from the chimney of 'Battle of Britain' Pacific No 34071 *201 Squadron*. *Michael E. Ware*

Centre left:
'Battle of Britain' Pacific No 34072 *257 Squadron* eases its boat train into the sidings at Folkestone Junction. 'P' class 0-6-0T No 31340 waits to take over at the rear end for the descent to the harbour on 24 July 1953. *W. A. Corkill*

Below:
Work stained 'Battle of Britain' Pacific No 34072 *257 Squadron* climbs the hill from Bickley to Bickley Junction on 27 July 1955 hauling a 15-coach 'Continental Express' from London Victoria to Dover Marine. One of many of Bulleid's Pacifics to end up at Barry, No 34072 has subsequently been preserved and is now fully operational again after years of restoration. *Brian Morrison*

Above:
'West Country' Pacific No 34091
Weymouth **enters Folkestone**
Central with a relief Victoria-
Folkestone Harbour boat train on
31 July 1955.
J. F. Davies/Photomatic 3266/Rail
Archive Stephenson

Right:
Bulleid 'Merchant Navy' No 35027
Port Line **heads a Dover-Victoria**
boat train past Folkestone
Junction on 7 June 1954. This
particular locomotive is one of a
number of the class to have
passed into preservation. Now
restored after many years at the
Barry scrapyard of Woodham
Bros, No 35027 has recently
returned to the main line on steam
specials. *T. G. Hepburn/Rail Archive*
Stephenson

Above:
'Schools' No 30934 *St Lawrence* passes Tonbridge with the 4.30pm Victoria-Folkestone boat train on 1 August 1960. *G. M. Kichenside*

Below:
The restored 'Golden Arrow' is near Westenhanger on 20 August 1949. 'West Country' Pacific No 34089, then unnamed, has a load of 10 Pullmans and two vans. *IAL*

Above:
A 'King Arthur' on a boat train working. 'N15' No 30773 *Sir Lavaine* **passes Queen Street crossing east of Paddock Wood with a down Continental express.** *W. A. Corkill*

Below:
Passengers from Folkestone Harbour were hauled up to the Junction where their main line locomotive awaited them by elderly South Eastern tank engines. Two Stirling Class R 0-6-0Ts of the South Eastern Railway and an 0-4-4T of the Wainwright period on the South Eastern & Chatham perform this task in 1949. *IAL*

Above:
Unrebuilt 'Battle of Britain' No 34067 Tangmere, which is currently undergoing restoration following preservation after many years at Barry, is pictured during its BR career near Weald with a down boat train on 13 May 1961. *D. M. C. Hepburne-Scott/Rail Archive Stephenson*

Below:
'Merchant Navy' No 35029 passes Knockholt with a down boat train. Note that the nameplates (the locomotive was to be named *Ellerman Lines*) are covered prior to unveiling. This locomotive was sold for scrap to Woodham Bros in South Wales. Rescued from the scrapyard, the locomotive was destined to be displayed in sectioned form in the National Railway Museum at York. *F. R. Hebron/Rail Archive Stephenson*

South Eastern Lines

The systems of the South Eastern Railway and the London, Chatham & Dover Railway were merged to form the South Eastern & Chatham Railway. This gave the SECR two routes through Kent, geographically separate for most of the way to the coast but with interconnections. The following illustrations are of steam on the former South Eastern route via Tonbridge and Ashford and connecting lines.

Above:
Rebuilt 'West Country' Pacific No 34100 *Appledore* **passes Chart Siding, near Ashford, with the down 'Golden Arrow' on 4 March 1961.** *John Head via Brian Stephenson*

Below:
Class N15 'King Arthur' *Sir Cador of Cornwall* **stands at Ashford on a down train on 11 August 1956.** *M. Mitchell*

Left:
'Battle of Britain' Pacific No 34089
***602 Squadron* leads its coaches**
through a typical Kent countryside
setting. *D. Sellman*

Early Crest
73A 1955 - 1959

Right:
Class L 4-4-0 No 31765 leaves
Paddock Wood for Ashford on a
stopping train on 20 September
1952. *K. W. Wightman*

Right:
The 4.58pm from Dover Priory to
Tonbridge passes Hawkesbury
Street Junction on 19 July 1958
behind Class L No 31758. *S. Creer*

Right:
Class D1 4-4-0 No 31727 leaves
the yard at Tonbridge with empty
stock in 1954. This was a Maunsell
rebuild of Wainwright's Class D.
P. Ransome-Wallis

Above:
'Schools' No 30918 *Hurstpierpoint* approaches Tonbridge with the down 'Man of Kent' on 1 September 1953. *W. A. Corkill*

Left:
'Schools' No 30925 *Cheltenham* on an up express freight near Tonbridge. *D. S. Murray*

Below left:
'N' class 2-6-0 No 31830 heads the Woking-Tonbridge 'Stone Train', conveying ballast from Meldon Quarries to the southeast district of the Southern Region. *Derek Cross*

Above right:
On 26 March 1953 a train for Redhill awaits departure from Tonbridge behind Class L No 31773. *Brian Morrison*

Right:
Class L 4-4-0 No 31771 works hard in pounding up Hildenborough Bank (on the approach to Sevenoaks) with an up semi-fast on 23 May 1955. *Brian Morrison*

Above:
'L1' No 31782 arrives at Stonegate with an up stopping train to Tonbridge on 7 July 1956. *G. Daniels*

Below:
'Schools' No 30936 *Cranleigh* winds out of Tonbridge in the summer of 1954 with the daily through train to Cannon Street via Redhill. *R. Russell*

Above:
BR Standard 2-6-4T No 80018 arrives at Tonbridge from Redhill with an SECR 'Birdcage' set on 19 August 1953.
J. Head

Below:
Class H 0-4-4T No 31523 pilots a push-pull set through Hildenborough cutting. *D. S. Murray*

Above left:
Class H 0-4-4T No 31553 heads away from Paddock Wood with the Hawkhurst branch train on 21 March 1960. *D. M. C. Hepburne-Scott/Rail Archive Stephenson*

Left:
On 28 May 1961 'D1' class No 31739 and 'E1' class 31067 double-headed a hop-pickers' special at Goudhurst on the Hawkhurst branch. As with so many aspects of life, these trains were to disappear with the closure of the rural lines throughout the country. *R. C. Riley*

Above right:
Last day on the Hawkhurst branch, 10 June 1961. Class C 0-6-0 No 31588 enters Cranbrook with the 4.25pm ex-Paddock Wood, strengthened to five coaches. *R. C. Riley*

Right:
Under British Railways the Kent & East Sussex line remained open for passengers until January 1954. In this 1953 picture Class A1X 'Terrier' No 32655 crosses the River Rother on a mixed train.
K. W. Wightman

Left:
Northernmost outpost of the K&ESR was Headcorn Junction, where the line met the ex-SECR main line to Ashford. At the K&ESR platform in the station on 27 July 1953 Class O1 0-6-0 No 31370 is photographed with its single-coach train. Although much of the old K&ESR survives (particularly if the preservationists fulfil their ambitious scheme to rebuild back to Robertsbridge), the section south from Headcorn to Tenterden has been completely abandoned. *R. C. Riley*

Below left:
The 8.50am Headcorn-Robertsbridge service shunts at Rolvenden on 28 November 1953. 'Terrier' No 32678 presides. *N. W. Sprinks*

Above right:
In August 1953 No 32655 arrives at Bodiam with a train from Robertsbridge. *Geoffrey F. Bannister*

Right:
K&ESR No 3 *Bodiam* is pictured at Rolvenden in March 1949. *D. A. Idle*

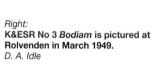

Below right:
Also at Rolvenden is the K&ESR Class P 0-6-0T. *LGRP*

Above:
A Sunday morning extra train from Hawkhurst to Paddock Wood arrives at Horsmonden hauled by Class C 0-6-0 No 31244. *Derek Cross*

Left:
The Hythe Branch train at Sandling Junction on 2 June 1951 with 'H' class 0-4-4T No 31322 waiting to depart for Hythe. *J. N. Young*

Below left
Hythe station on 2 June 1951 with No 31322 ready to return to Sandling Junction. *J. N. Young*

Above right:
'Schools' class 4-4-0 No 30929 *Malvern* arrives at Shorncliffe with a London-Dover train c1954.
T. G. Hepburn/Rail Archive Stephenson

Right:
In June 1954 'H' class 0-4-4T No 31531 was photographed with an up parcels train at Shorncliffe.
T. G. Hepburn/Rail Archive Stephenson

Above:
'Schools' No 30927 *Clifton* arrives at Ashford on 27 July 1960 with the 11.46am from Charing Cross. The bridge and building in this picture were demolished during reconstruction of Ashford station. *Dennis C. Ovenden*

Below:
The 1.15pm from Charing Cross to Folkestone and Dover passes Petts Wood on 10 May 1952 with 'Battle of Britain' No 34078 *222 Squadron* leaving a smoke trail. *A. A. Sellman*

Above:
**The 9.47am Ashford-Margate service headed by Class H
0-4-4T No 31326 approaches the junction with the recently-
opened connecting spur between the SER and LCDR lines
at Canterbury on 26 April 1953.** *J. Head*

Below:
**Rebuilt 'West Country' Pacific No 34001 *Exeter* passes Petts
Wood with the 9.10am Charing Cross-Ramsgate train on
14 September 1959.**
B. C. Bending

Above:
Shakespeare Cliff, Dover, is the setting for Class N No 31404 on an up vans train in April 1952.
P. Ransome-Wallis

Left:
Class U 2-6-0 No 31638 approaches Tonbridge on a train from Ashford on 11 April 1951.
G. H. Robin

Below left:
'Schools' No 30908 *Westminster* hurries through Hildenborough cutting with a train for the coast.
D.S. Murray

Above right:
A down empty stock train passes Ashford in the charge of 'Schools' No 30921 *Shrewsbury*. *Dennis C. Ovenden*

Right:
Work pauses to watch 'West Country' Pacific No 34097 *Holsworthy* approaching Ashford with a down Kent Coast train.
W. A. Corkill

Above:
Class N 2-6-0 No 31848 leaves Dover with the 3pm ex-Ramsgate mail train to Cannon Street via Redhill on 8 August 1953. *M. W. Hamilton*

Left:
The 'Birkenhead' at Redhill, combining portions from Ramsgate, Folkestone, Brighton and Hastings to Birmingham, Chester and Birkenhead. The locomotive is 'U' class 2-6-0 No 1618. *H. M. Madgwick*

Above:
'Schools' 30919 *Harrow* takes the 2.42pm from Margate to Cannon Street round the Minster loop. The train was routed via Dover and Redhill. *W. A. Corkill*

Right:
Rebuilt 'West Country' Pacific No 34001 *Exeter* heads a down Cannon Street-Ramsgate train near Reculver. *P. Ransome-Wallis*

Right:
An up Ramsgate excursion leaves Sandwich behind 'Schools' No 30936 *Cranleigh*. *P. Ransome-Wallis*

Above:
'Battle of Britain' No 34080 *74 Squadron* blasts up the hill out of Dumpton Park with the Sunday Pullman, 4.48pm ex-Birchington, to Victoria via Ramsgate. *W. A. Corkill*

Left:
'L1' No 31786 passes Petts Wood in early BR days with a down train. *E. R. Wethersett*

Right:
BR Standard 4-6-0 No 75067 arrives at Folkestone Junction with an up parcels train from Dover in August 1957. It has just passed through the short Folkestone tunnel. *J. K. Morton*

Above:
'H' class 0-4-4T No 31276 awaits departure from New Romney with a branch line train to the junction at Appledore in June 1954. The ex-SECR branch lost its passenger services on 6 March 1967, although much of the line remains today to serve the nuclear power station at Dungeness. *T. G. Hepburn/Rail Archive Stephenson*

Left:
Having just departed from Dover Priory with a train for Margate, the crew of 'Schools' class 4-4-0 No 30929 *Malvern* prepare to enter Guston tunnel. *T. G. Hepburn/Rail Archive Stephenson*

The North Kent Coast

The London, Chatham & Dover fought first for a share of Continental traffic. The opening of a branch from Faversham on the Dover line to Whitstable in 1860 was the first step towards serving a string of resorts along the North Kent Coast.

A special to Chatham storms out of Broadstairs at 10.30pm on 18 September 1952 with excursionists returning from the Margate illuminations.
A. W. V. Mace

Left:
Lettered tiles on the frontage of Blackfriars station offered a selection of interesting destinations to travellers availing themselves of the services of the London, Chatham & Dover Railway. The tiles have been preserved in the concourse of the rebuilt station. *British Railways*

Below:
'Schools' No 30935 *Sevenoaks* climbs Sole Street bank on 21 August 1954 with the 2.15pm train from Ramsgate to Victoria. *S. C. Nash*

Above:
A Victoria-Margate train passing Beckenham Junction on 6 June 1954 is headed by 'Schools' No 30914 *Eastbourne.*
S. Creer

Below:
A 'Q' class 0-6-0 heads a down excursion between Bickley Junction and St Mary Cray in a cutting which is being widened to take two additional tracks for the Kent Coast electrification. *D. A. Bosomworth*

Class N15 'King Arthur' No 30764 *Sir Gawain* takes it easy on a hot summer day in July 1952 with a Margate return excursion near Teynham. *P. Ransome-Wallis*

Pictured on the Chislehurst-St Mary Cray loop on 13 July 1951, Class D1 No 31741 was heading for Dover with a train of vans from London Bridge. *Brian Morrison*

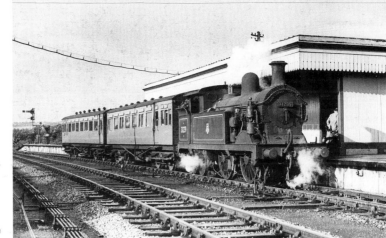

Right:
Dunton Green was the junction for the branch to Westerham with its intermediate stations at Chevening Halt and Brasted. On 9 June 1959 'H' class 0-4-4T No 31239 waits to depart for Westerham with a two-coach train formed of ex-SECR steam railmotor coaches.
D. M. C. Hepburne-Scott/Rail Archive Stephenson

Centre right:
'Schools' class 4-4-0 No 30903 *Charterhouse* is pictured at the head of the 2.25pm service from Charing Cross to Tonbridge and Hastings passing Chelsfield on 22 May 1952. *C. R. L. Coles*

Below:
'H' class No 31308 departs from Brasted with a Westerham branch service on 8 October 1961. At this point the M25 motorway runs along the trackbed of the now-closed branch, obliterating this scene of rural charm. Note the wonderfully insignificant direction board for the station; it's almost as though BR was ashamed that it possessed a station at this point!
Brian Stephenson

Left:

A third 'H' class 0-4-4T is seen on the branch; No 31530 is seen at Westerham terminus prior to returning to Dunton Green on 8 October 1961. The branch by this time had but weeks to go before closure; passenger services were withdrawn on 30 October 1961. *Brian Stephenson*

Below left:

'Schools' class 4-4-0 No 30914 *Eastbourne* **heads a Victoria service at Shortlands.** *D. Sellman*

Above right:

Wainwright 'H' class 0-4-4T No 31239 approaches journey's end on 26 march, with the 9.54am auto-train from Westerham to Dunton Green. *Brian Morrison*

Centre right:

Chatham arrivals — rebuilt 'West Country' Pacific No 34027 *Taw Valley* **enters the station with a Cannon Street-Ramsgate express in April 1959.** *P. Ransome-Wallis*

Below right:

'Schools' No 30901 *Winchester* **arrives with an up Kent Coast express in the same month.** *P. Ransome-Wallis*

Above:
'L' class 4-4-0 No 31780 climbs away from Herne Bay with a Ramsgate train on a Wednesday afternoon in August 1957. *Brian Coates*

Below:
The up Saturday 'Kentish Belle' near Herne Bay in August 1955 with 'Schools' No 30912 *Downside*. *P. Ransome-Wallis*

Above:
Another 'Kentish Belle' picture of the same period, this time near Ramsgate and a different 'Schools' — No 30917 Ardingly. *P. Ransome-Wallis*

Below:
BR Standard Class 2 2-6-2T No 84028 is seen shunting coaches at Margate after arriving with a train from Ashford on 28 March 1959. *R. C. Riley*

The interior of Ramsgate (74B) shed in the immediate post-Nationalisation years. Although 'J' class 0-6-4T No 31595 has acquired a BR smokebox number, 'Battle of Britain' No 34068 *Kenley* is still in Southern livery, with its new number painted on the buffer beam. The anonymous locomotive in the background clearly displays its pre-Nationalisation ownership. *David Watkin/Rail Archive Stephenson*

Right:
**BR Standard 4-6-0 No 75068
leaves Ramsgate with an
excursion from Dartford to Deal.**
P. Ransome-Wallis

Right:
**BR Standard 2-6-2T No 84029
climbs Blacksole Bank with a
Faversham-Ramsgate train in
September 1958.** *P. Ransome-
Wallis*

Right:
**Class N15 'King Arthur' 4-6-0
No 30802 *Sir Durnore* leaves
Newington (between Rainham and
Sittingbourne) with a Kent Coast-
Victoria train in February 1959.**
P. Ransome-Wallis

Left:
'N15' No 30795 *Sir Dinadan* has been paired with an eight-wheel tender in this photograph, taken on 4 May 1958, of the 10.40am Ramsgate-Victoria train leaving Faversham. *S. Creer*

Below left:
'N15' 30769 *Sir Balan* lifts the 3.28pm Dover Priory-Victoria up Sole Street bank on 11 April 1955. *S. C. Nash*

Above:
The 12.45pm Southwark-Dover Marine Sidings empty Continental produce vans train is near Snowdown Colliery with 'N15' No 30776 *Sir Galagars* in charge on 23 May 1955. *R. A. King*

Below:
Faversham based Ivatt Class 2 No 41312 heads a Dover Priory to Faversham train, seen leaving Lydden in September 1952. *P. Ransome Wallis*

Above:
A Saturdays Only Victoria-Ramsgate express is near Teynham in August 1956 with 'N1' 2-6-0 No 31822.
P. Ransome-Wallis

Below:
'N1' 2-6-0 No 31878, a Hither Green engine, works a down excursion near Teynham. Locomotives from Hither Green were often seen on passenger workings such as this in the summer. *P. Ransome-Wallis*

Above:
The 2-6-0 on an up Ramsgate express leaving Herne Bay in July 1956 is Class N No 31410.
P. Ransome-Wallis

Right:
Class D1 4-4-0 No 31492 heads an up fruit special between Teynham and Sittingbourne on 29 June 1952. *Donald Kelk*

Top:
In the last days before the live rail, 'N' class 2-6-0 No 31811 shuts off steam for a check near St Mary Cray with a Victoria-Ramsgate train on 13 June 1959. *P. H. Groom*

Above:
A down slow train with Class L 4-4-0 No 31765 passes a lineside notice announcing the approach of electrification. *P. Ransome-Wallis*

Above:
Class O1 0-6-0 No 31065 approaches Golgotha Tunnel from Eythorne on the East Kent Section. *J. H. Aston*

Below:
'O1' No 1434 is nearing Eythorne on a Shepherds Well-Tilmanstone Colliery train. *A. W. Burges*

Top:
An unusual duty for an East Kent line 'O1': No 31065 rounds the connecting spur at Shepherds Well on 6 May 1960 with the Chipman Chemical Co's weedkilling train, heading for Tilmanstone. *Derek Cross*

Above:
An 'O1' has attached its train and is ready to leave Tilmanstone Colliery. *J. H. Aston*

Above:
East Kent Section 0-6-0, formerly SR No 1383, at Shepherds Well in 1947. *LGRP*

Below:
'O1' No 1381 at Folkestone Junction in 1947. *LGRP*

Selected Shed Allocations

Faversham (73E)
as at 1959

Class C	31242, 31255, 31256, 31268, 31298, 31481, 31714, 31715
Class D1	31494, 31505, 31509
Class H	31503
Class L	31765, 31766, 31768
Class N	31850, 31852
Class U1	31892, 31893, 31903
Class 2 (Ivatt)	41308, 41309, 41310, 41311, 41312, 41313

Ramsgate (74B)
as at 1959

'Schools'	30910 *Merchant Taylors*, 30911 *Dover*, 30912 *Downside*, 30913 *Christ's Hospital*, 30914 *Eastbourne*, 30916 *Whitgift*, 30917 *Ardingly*, 30918 *Hurstpierpoint*, 30919 *Harrow*, 30920 *Rugby*, 30921 *Shrewsbury*, 30922 *Marlborough*
Class C	31004, 31245, 31252, 31271, 31592
Class H	31324, 31326, 31500
Class L	31764, 31775, 31779, 31780, 31781
'West Country'	34016 *Bodmin*, 34017 *Ilfracombe*, 34021 *Dartmoor*, 34022 *Exmoor*, 34025 *Whimple*, 34026 *Yes Tor*, 34027 *Taw Valley*, 34037 *Clovelly*
'Battle of Britain'	34078 *222 Squadron*
Class 2 (BR)	84025, 84026, 84027, 84028, 84029

**Allhallows-on-Sea station was built to serve a planned
resort on the south shore of the Thames Estuary.** *LGRP*

Estuary Lines

The shores of the estuaries of the Thames and the Medway were served by branches north of the main line to Dover and the Kent Coast.

Above:
The Allhallows branch train leaving Gravesend on 20 June 1952. 'H' class 0-4-4T No 31658 is propelling its push-pull set out of the station. *Brian Morrison*

Below:
Less than a week later, on 26 June 1952, sister locomotive No 31295 was the motive power for the Allhallows branch train. It is seen at Gravesend Central awaiting departure. *Brian Morrison*

Above:
'H' class No 31553 takes water at Gravesend on an Allhallows train on 26 May 1960. *J. A. V. Smallwood*

Below:
Sharnal Street station on the Allhallows branch on 26 May 1960. The locomotive is Class H No 31553.
J. A. V. Smallwood

Above:
In this view of No 31662 taking water at Allhallows the hotel built to welcome a holiday traffic that failed to materialise is seen beyond the station in the background.
  P. Ransome-Wallis

Below:
Class R 0-4-4T No 31662 leaves Sharnal Street on a Gravesend train in September 1952. *P. Ransome Wallis*

Steam Still Active

A selection of photographs of steam still in action in Kent and Sussex

Closure of the East Grinstead-Lewes line in 1958 turned out in fact to be the dawn of a new beginning. A society first called the Lewes to East Grinstead Railway Preservation Society was formed and at a meeting on 14 June 1959 it was decided that effort should be concentrated on reopening the Sheffield Park-Horsted Keynes section. The Bluebell Railway Preservation Society was formally constituted. In contrast to the large locomotive stock of today, the Society had only two working steam locomotives to begin operations. They were the A1X 'Terrier' No 55 *Stepney* and SER 'P' class No 323, now proudly named *Bluebell*. The inaugural train on the new Bluebell Railway ran on 7 August 1960. The Bluebell Railway was the first ex-British Rail standard gauge preserved line in Britain.

At first the aim of the Society was to recreate a typical steam-worked rural section of the LBSC. Soon much wider objectives were set. A Great Western 'Dukedog', a BR Standard 4-6-0, a Southern Region 'West Country' Pacific and an ex-LSWR Adams 4-4-2T are but a few examples of the variety of motive power to be seen in operation from time to time, often supplemented by visiting locomotives.

In Kent a preservation society was formed immediately after closure of the Kent & East Sussex Railway to passengers in January 1954. The Robertsbridge-Tenterden section remained open for goods traffic and occasional hop pickers' specials until 1961. The preservation group had hoped to reopen the line from Tenterden to Robertsbridge. The attempt failed but after a protracted legal battle the section from Tenterden to Bodiam, 3½ miles short of the connection with BR at Robertsbridge, was saved. After much effort by volunteers the section from Tenterden to Rolvenden was passed for traffic in 1974 and passenger working began. The 'Terrier' *Bodiam* had been transferred by BR to the Hayling Island branch where it worked until the line was closed in 1963. It was then purchased privately and placed on permanent loan with the restored Kent & East Sussex Railway. Here it has worked alongside another 'Terrier', *Sutton*, and a variety of other steam power.

In the north of the county the age of industrial steam is recalled by the Sittingbourne & Kemsley Light Railway. The line was built to link a paper mill at Sittingbourne with a wharf on an inlet of the Swale. A larger mill was built at Kemsley in 1924 at approximately the mid-point of the line. The mills were taken over by the Bowater Group in 1948. Steam operations continued but an economic study in 1965 concluded that the mills would be better served by a fleet of lorries. Bowaters then closed the line, but after consultation with the Locomotive Club of Great Britain handed over the section between Kemsley Down and Sittingbourne for preservation. The company also donated six tank engines with the spark-arresting chimneys which had been fitted for them to work in a paper-making environment. With other motive power acquired since, the Sittingbourne & Kemsley Light Railway keeps alive the sights and sounds of industrial steam.

Above:
The Bluebell's Standard Class 4MT 4-6-0 No 75027 with a train for Horsted Keynes on Freshfield Bank. *D. A. Idle*

Below:
An S&KLR train from Kemsley Down approaches its destination hauled by Kerr Stuart 0-4-2ST *Leader*.
Brian Morrison

Above:
Visiting the Kent & East Sussex Railway on loan from the North Yorkshire Moors in August 1992, Great Western '56xx' 0-6-2T No 6619 runs into Wittersham Road with a train from Tenterden. *Brian Morrison*

Above right:
At Tenterden on Ian Allan Day, 12 July 1992, Class A1X Terrier No 10 Sutton displays a 'Railway World' headboard while working a Kent & East Sussex service for Northiam. *Brian Morrison*

Right:
Bagnall 0-6-2T Superb approaches Kemsley Down from Sittingbourne on the S&KLR. *Brian Morrison*

The Romney, Hythe & Dymchurch Railway's 'Canadian' Pacific *Doctor Syn* approaches Botolph's Bridge Road with the 11.20am Hythe to Dungeness. *P. H. Groom*

Above:
RH&D Pacific *Southern Maid* approaches Hythe with the 3pm arrival from Dungeness. *P. H. Groom*